VOLUME TWO

The Screwtape Letters

Paradise Lost

Confessions

The Pursuit of God

A Taste of the Classics

SUMMARIZED BY KEN BOA, PHD

Biblica™

Biblica Publishing
We welcome your questions and comments.

USA   1820 Jet Stream Drive, Colorado Springs, CO 80921
        www.authenticbooks.com
India   Logos Bhavan, Medchal Road, Jeedimetla Village, Secunderabad
        500 055, A.P.

A Taste of the Classics, Volume Two
ISBN-13: 978-1-93406-811-3

Copyright © 2010 by Kenneth D. Boa

12 11 10 / 6 5 4 3 2 1

Published in 2010 by Biblica
A catalog record for this book is available through the Library of Congress.

Printed in the United States of America

CONTENTS

PREFACE

Christians have a rich heritage of devout saints and brilliant thinkers, many of whom have left us their writings. Those with access to these writings have a treasure trove to help them along their journey of faith.

However, many of us lead frenetic lives that don't leave time for reflection, let alone engagement with some of the best Christian literature from across the generations. Dr. Kenneth Boa has helpfully summarized a number of these classics to give you a taste of what you may be missing. You may find deep refreshment in this book. Or, as with any sampler platter, you may discover a morsel you would delight to savor again. Perhaps you could then pick up the original work with a framework already in place to help you immediately engage the classic. Regardless of how you use this book, we hope your faith will be enriched through the considerable insights of generations before us.

A note on method: Dr. Boa cites numerous passages from each book. Because he proceeds through a book from beginning to end, we have chosen not to cite page numbers. This will create a more pleasant reading experience for you, and you will be able to locate passages from each book by the cues the author gives here.

Since the primary audience for this book is American, we have changed spellings to what is commonly accepted in the United States. However, we have left the original style and capitalization for each author. There are some points where authors used dubious capitalization, but we have chosen not to note them (using [sic]), again for ease of reading. Poetry is usually set in prose, for the sake of space. In this case, the initial capital letter in a line of poetry has been lowercased. The following editions are cited in this book:

Lewis, C. S. *The Screwtape Letters*. New York: HarperCollins, 2001. All unattributed quotations in the "Introduction" and "Preface" are taken from edition: New York: Macmillan, 1961.

Milton, John. *Paradise Lost*, eds. Stephen Orgel and Jonathan Goldberg. New York: Oxford University Press, 2008.

Augustine. *Confessions*, trans. David McDuff. London: Penguin, 1961.

Tozer, A. W. *The Pursuit of God*. Radford, VA: Wilder Publications, 2008.

Special thanks are due to Cindy Barnwell, who helped Dr. Boa edit and enrich the manuscript for publication.

C. S. LEWIS

The Screwtape Letters

Introduction

The writings of C. S. Lewis resonate well with many of us because of his keen insights, his broad imagination, and his wonderful ability to distill complex theological concepts. Certainly, all these elements are evident in his little book *The Screwtape Letters*, although in his preface, Lewis humorously provided additional motivations for the book's popularity, explaining, "It is . . . the sort that gravitates towards spare bedrooms, there to live a life of undisturbed tranquility in company with [a variety of unknown books]." He went on to say, "Sometimes it is bought for even more humiliating reasons. A lady whom I knew discovered that the pretty little probationer who filled her hot-water bottle in the hospital had read *Screwtape*. She also discovered why. 'You see,' said the girl, 'we were warned that at interviews, after the real, technical questions are over, matrons and people sometimes ask about your general interests. The best thing is to say you've read something. So they gave us a list of about ten books that usually go down pretty well. . . .' 'And you chose *Screwtape?*' 'Well, of course; it was the shortest.'"

Evidently, it was around July 1940 that Lewis first conceived the idea for this work of fiction. He wrote a letter to his brother, Warney—who had been evacuated from Dunkirk and was residing in a camp in Cardiff, Wales—concerning Hitler's charismatic radio speeches. Somewhat sheepishly, he acknowledged, "I don't know if I'm weaker than other people: but it is a positive revelation to me how *while the speech lasts* it is impossible not to waver just a little. I should be useless as a schoolmaster or a policeman. Statements which I *know* to be untrue all but convince me, at any rate for the moment, if only the man says them unflinchingly" (*The Collected Letters of C. S. Lewis, Vol. 2* [New York: HarperCollins, 2004], 425).

And so Lewis was still thinking about Hitler's momentary persuasiveness when, on Sunday, July 21, he attended a service at Holy Trinity Church, near his home east of Oxford. It was a Communion service, and he wrote, in that same letter to his brother, "Before the service was over—one could wish these things came more seasonably—I was struck by an idea for a book which I think might be both useful and entertaining. It would be called *As one Devil to Another* and would consist of letters from an elderly retired devil to a young devil who has just started work on his first 'patient'" (426). His idea was to examine the psychology of temptation from the point of view of the tempter rather than the tempted.

By Christmas of 1940 he had completed this work. This was before his popular radio broadcast talks, which were later combined into *Mere Christianity*.

In *The Screwtape Letters*, we have thirty-one letters on the art of temptation, all written by Screwtape, an elderly devil in hell's civil service. They are addressed to a junior devil—Screwtape's nephew—named Wormwood, who has just been put in charge of an unnamed young man, his first "patient," whose soul he is trying to secure. The book's purpose is to examine the daily motivations and decisions of this ordinary man from the viewpoint of hell and thereby reveal truth through this very unusual perspective. The events in the life of this patient are not meant to be of great interest; they only serve to demonstrate the immortal consequences of seemingly insignificant choices in the daily life of every person.

Lewis's Preface

The Screwtape Letters is a very compact book that lends itself to multiple readings because of its rich insights. Before I go into the material itself, I want to mention just a few thoughts from Lewis's preface, written some time after the book received such remarkable welcome and praise. He dedicated the book to J. R. R. Tolkien, who was his very close friend. (Tolkien and Hugo Dyson, another professor at Oxford, were the two men most influential in Lewis's conversion to Christianity.) Lewis wrote in the preface, "There are two equal and opposite errors into which our race can fall about the devils. One is to disbelieve in their existence. The other is to believe, and to feel an excessive and unhealthy interest in them. They themselves are equally pleased by both errors and hail a materialist or a magician with the same delight."

That is an important and perceptive observation. Satan does not care if we completely repudiate and reject the idea of spiritual warfare, or if, on the other hand, we become consumed with it, for either error provides Satan with a foothold. Lewis then continued, "Readers are advised to remember that the devil is a liar. Not everything that Screwtape says should be assumed to be true even from his own angle." Lewis made these cautionary remarks to remind the reader of the subtlety and seductiveness of temptation. Sometime later he wrote a second preface, referencing the fact that the letters of Screwtape had appeared in a newspaper that had since gone out of business. Lewis noted, "I hope they did not hasten its death, but they certainly lost it one reader. A country clergyman wrote to the editor, withdrawing his subscription on the ground that 'much of the advice given in these letters seemed to him not only erroneous but positively diabolical.'" Obviously, the clergyman had missed the whole point of the letters.

After the initial remarkable reception the book enjoyed, Lewis found himself the recipient of many questions about the work. The most common question was whether he believed in a literal Devil. In a second preface, Lewis answered this question:

> Now, if by "the Devil" you mean a power opposite to God and, like God, self-existent from all eternity, the answer is certainly No. There

is no uncreated being except God. God has no opposite. No being could attain a "perfect badness" opposite to the perfect goodness of God; for when you have taken away every kind of good thing (intelligence, will, memory, energy, and existence itself) there would be none of him left.

The proper question is whether I believe in devils. I do. That is to say, I believe in angels, and I believe that some of these, by the abuse of their free will, have become enemies to God and, as a corollary, to us. These we may call devils. They do not differ in nature from good angels, but their nature is depraved. *Devil* is the opposite of *angel* only as Bad Man is the opposite of Good Man. Satan, the leader or dictator of devils, is the opposite, not of God, but of Michael.

This is a very important observation. Many people erroneously suppose there is some sort of theological dualism in which Satan is the counterpart of God, yet nothing could be further from the truth. Satan is, arguably, the most powerful being God ever created, but he holds no candle to God's authority and power. He is, in fact, a created being and therefore accountable to God and bound by the limitations of finitude. Furthermore, Scripture reveals his ultimate demise. Revelation 20 describes the doom of Satan, when he will be cast into the lake of fire. Lewis asserted, "It should be (but it is not) unnecessary to add that a belief in angels, whether good or evil, does not mean a belief in either as they are represented in art and literature." There devils have been depicted, he explained, "with bats' wings and good angels with birds' wings, not because anyone holds that moral deterioration would be likely to turn feathers into membrane, but because most men like birds better than bats. They are given wings at all in order to suggest the swiftness of unimpeded intellectual energy. They are given human form because man is the only rational creature we know. . . . These forms are not only symbolical but were always known to be symbolical by reflective people."

Lewis continued the discussion: "In the plastic arts these symbols have steadily degenerated. Fra Angelico's angels carry in their face and gesture the peace and authority of Heaven." If we go to medieval work, we will see angels with authority, but this changes in later art. "Later come the chubby infantile nudes of Raphael; finally the soft, slim, girlish, and consolatory angels of nineteenth century art, shapes so feminine that they avoid being voluptuous only by their total insipidity. . . . They are a pernicious symbol."

"In Scripture the visitation of an angel is always alarming; it has to begin by saying 'Fear not,'" because the visitation is such a terrifying event. We may think we want to see an angel, but the Bible represents these situations as very unsettling for the people involved. However, Lewis noted that "the Victorian angel looks as if it were going to say, 'There, there.'" Lewis was highly critical of a Victorian and modern representation of the angelic realm that reduced the holy to merely insipid and degraded images of the biblical model.

Literary symbols have also changed over the centuries. Lewis argued that Dante's representations are best because

"Before his angels we sink in awe. His devils, as Ruskin rightly remarked, in their rage, spite, and obscenity, are far more like what reality must be than anything in Milton." Then Lewis addressed the issue of humor, as well, observing, "Humor involves a sense of proportion and a power of seeing yourself from the outside. Whatever else we attribute to beings who sinned through pride, we must not attribute this. Satan, said Chesterton, fell through force of gravity."

Lewis continued, "We must picture Hell as a state where everyone is perpetually concerned about his own dignity and advancement, where everyone has a grievance, and where everyone lives the deadly and serious passions of envy, self-importance, and resentment." Once again, Lewis labored to clarify misconceptions regarding sin. Humor is a gift of God and reflects his divine nature. It can neither be enjoyed by the damned, nor is it fitting that we be entertained by that which offends God and sent Christ to the cross. Lewis's use of sardonic humor in this little work does not glorify or minimize sin but rather spotlights it, providing invaluable lessons for the reader.

Lewis continued, "My symbol for Hell is something like the bureaucracy of a police state or the offices of a thoroughly nasty business concern." He then elaborated on that idea:

> It enabled me, by earthly parallels, to picture an official society held together entirely by fear and greed. On the surface, manners are normally suave. Rudeness to one's superiors would obviously be suicidal; rudeness to one's equals might put them on their guard before you were ready to spring your mine.

For of course "Dog eat dog" is the principle of the whole organization. Everyone wishes everyone else's discrediting, demotion, and ruin; everyone is an expert in the confidential report, the pretended alliance, the stab in the back. Over all this their good manners, their expressions of grave respect, their "tributes" to one another's invaluable services form a thin crust. Every now and then it gets punctured, and the scalding lava of their hatred spurts out.

All of us have probably noted parallels in human relationships not far removed from Lewis's imagery. He clarified the two motives that, as he understood them, devils possess. Lewis surmised that their primary motive is fear of punishment and that their second is a kind of hunger: "I feign that devils can, in a spiritual sense, eat one another; and us. Even in human life we have seen the passion to dominate, almost to digest, one's fellow; to make his whole intellectual and emotional life merely an extension of one's own."

Lewis employed this theme of the consuming nature of evil throughout this work, as well as in others. For example, in *Perelandra*, the middle book in his science fiction trilogy, Lewis described the voracious appetite of hell through the destruction of the novel's villain, Weston, who gives both mind and body over to evil forces. Through the protagonist, Lewis universalizes Weston's downfall: "There was, no doubt, a confusion of persons in damnation: what Pantheists falsely hoped of Heaven bad men really received in Hell. They were melted down into their Master, as a lead soldier slips down and loses his shape in the ladle over the gas ring. The question whether Satan, or the one whom Satan has digested, is acting on any given occasion, has in the long run no clear signifi-cance" ([New York: Scribner, 1996], 173). He depicted hell as a distortion of love, where "they recognize it as hunger. But there the hunger is more ravenous, and a fuller satisfac-tion is possible. There, I suggest, the stronger spirit—there are perhaps no bodies to impede the operation—can really and irrevocably suck the weaker into itself and permanently gorge its own being on the weaker's outraged individuality." He further wrote, "It is for this that Satan desires all his own followers and all the sons of Eve and all the host of Heaven. His dream is of the day when all shall be inside him and all that says 'I' can say it only through him."

Lewis went on to say, "God turns tools into servants and servants into sons, so that they may be at last reunited to Him in the perfect freedom of a love offered from the height of the utter individualities which he has liberated them to be." Rather than devouring us, our service to God becomes something that completely frees us, so that we still enjoy the I-thou relationship. This significantly contrasts the Eastern-religion image of virtually being devoured by or absorbed into the ocean of being. According to that worldview, people lose both individuality and consciousness in a kind of spiri-tual annihilation.

Therefore, Lewis used the concept of spiritual cannibal-ism among the devils in order to contrast Satan's goals with God's goals. Lewis's devils possess no conception of God's true love. In damnation selfishness obliterates love, and insa-tiable appetite replaces relationship.

Lewis employed a few coined terms in this work that

could be somewhat confusing without explanation. For example, he referred to a "lowerarchy" as opposed to "hierarchy" among the world of devils. The epithet "Our Father Below" refers to Satan, while the "Enemy" refers to God. Because of the atypical point of view of the work, there is an inversion of definitions that the reader must keep in mind.

Two other comments from Lewis are worth mentioning at this point. Many people assumed that his letters "were the ripe fruit of many years' study in moral and ascetic theology. They forgot that there is an equally reliable, though less credible, way of learning how temptation works. 'My heart'—I need no other's—'showeth me the wickedness of the ungodly.'" Here Lewis humbly explained that the wealth of insights in his book merely required examination of his own nature. He went on to describe how we can, in fact, "twist one's mind into the diabolical attitude," but after a while, he noted, "it was not fun, or not for long. The strain produced a sort of spiritual cramp."

In other words, this work was, as he explained through Screwtape, "all dust, grit, thirst, and itch. Every trace of beauty, freshness, and geniality had to be excluded." Its creation almost smothered Lewis, and he determined not to write any more such letters, even though people clamored for them. Years later, however, he did finally write one additional letter. When the *Saturday Evening Post* asked for another letter, he penned "Screwtape Proposes a Toast."

This reminds me of a process I went through when I wrote *Cults, World Religions and the Occult*. Frankly, of all my books, that one was the most difficult to write because I had to use the primary sources in my research of world religions and the occult. After a while it was indeed a "spiritual cramp" for me, as well. I could hardly wait to finish that book and refrain from exposing myself to demonic ideas. Apart from that volume and a series of tapes I produced, I have not immersed myself again in that kind of literature. Like Lewis, I found it spiritually repugnant.

First Letter

The first letter from Screwtape introduces the idea of argument and warns Wormwood against the use of argument in his temptations and offers a very telling critique of contemporary culture. Screwtape states, "It sounds as if you supposed that *argument* was the way to keep him out of the Enemy's clutches. That might have been so if he had lived a few centuries earlier. At that time the humans still knew pretty well when a thing was proved and when it was not; and if it was proved they really believed it. They still connected thinking with doing and were prepared to alter their way of life as the result of a chain of reasoning. But what with the weekly press and other such weapons we have largely altered that." Screwtape alludes to mass communications, and today he would likely add television to the list, as well. He goes on to assert, "Your man has been accustomed, ever since he was a boy, to have a dozen incompatible philosophies dancing about together inside his head. He doesn't think of doctrines as primarily 'true' or 'false,' but as 'academic' or 'practical,' 'outworn' or 'contemporary,' 'conventional' or 'ruthless.' Jargon, not argument, is your best ally in keeping him from the Church. Don't waste time trying to make him think that materialism is *true*! Make him think it is strong, or stark, or courageous—that is the philosophy of the future. That's the sort of thing he cares about."

The lack of clear thinking is even more widespread now than in 1940. It is not vigorous, well-reasoned argumentation that persuades, but jargon and clever terminology. These persuasive elements are evident in television commercials. I tell parents that one of the most surprising exercises is to record three hours of prime-time television on a major network and then fast-forward through the shows, viewing only the commercials and pausing to discuss them. I then suggest that the parents consider what basic desires each commercial appeals to. Such an exercise would reveal that money, sex, and power are the three main marketing tools. The lust of the flesh, the lust of the eyes, and the boastful pride of life are used repeatedly in order to sell products. Commercials are full of association but very little content. We are a people who are often governed by our baser instincts.

Screwtape goes on to say, "How enslaved they are to the pressure of the ordinary." He describes a former patient who, as he was reading in the British Museum, began to think sensibly and question his beliefs. Screwtape thwarted contemplation by quickly advising his patient: "'Much better come back after lunch and go into it with a fresh mind.' . . . Once he was in the street the battle was won. I showed him a newsboy shouting the midday paper, and a No. 73 bus going past, and before he reached the bottom of the steps . . . a healthy dose of 'real life' . . . was enough to show him that all 'that sort of thing' just couldn't be true. . . . He is now safe in Our Father's house." The reality and ordinariness of things can often obscure the deeper realities of life. In other words, a person can find it all but impossible to believe in the unfamiliar while the familiar is right before his or her eyes.

Second Letter

In the second letter, Screwtape discusses the church, arguing to the junior demon that "one of our great allies at present is the Church itself." He continues, "I do not mean the Church as we see her spread out through all time and space and rooted in eternity, terrible as an army with banners." Here Lewis offered a wonderful image of the true church, but that is not the subject of Screwtape's letter, for he goes on to admit "that, I confess, is a spectacle which makes our boldest tempters uneasy. But fortunately it is quite invisible to these humans." What he addresses instead are the man-made religious expressions and institutions, with all their foibles, hypocrisy, and annoying traditions and requirements.

Later in the letter, he talks about "the transition from dreaming aspiration to laborious doing." Screwtape acknowledges that "the Enemy takes this risk because He has a curious fantasy of making all these disgusting little human vermin into what He calls His 'free' lovers and servants—'sons' is the word He uses, with His inveterate love of degrading the whole spiritual world by unnatural liaisons with the two-legged animals."

He finds it particularly loathsome that God seeks their freedom and that "He . . . refuses to carry them, by their mere affections and habits, to any of the goals which He sets before them." Here Lewis contrasted evil's usurpation of the mind with God's gifts of will and reason. This becomes a very important concept. Later on in this letter Screwtape advises Wormwood, "All you then have to do is keep out of [your patient's] mind the question 'If I, being what I am, can consider that I am in some sense a Christian, why should the different vices of those people in the next pew prove that their religion is mere hypocrisy and convention?'" In other words, the real question would be, If I know what my heart is like, how can I condemn these people? Screwtape writes, "You may ask whether it is possible to keep such an obvious thought from occurring even to a human mind. It is, Wormwood, it is! Handle him properly and it simply won't come into his head." This second letter emphasizes the dangers of the abandonment of reason and judgmental hypocrisy.

Third Letter

The third letter includes a discussion about the patient's mother. The demonic strategy employed here—and it is one of the most elementary duties—is to keep the young patient's mind focused on the irritating qualities of his mother while remaining oblivious of his own flaws: "Aggravate that most useful human characteristic, the horror and neglect of the obvious. You must bring him to a condition in which he can practice self-examination for an hour without discovering any of those facts about himself which are perfectly clear to anyone who has ever lived in the same house with him or worked in the same office." In other words, if Satan can keep us away from hard reality and focus us on our own vain imaginations, then our deception is virtually complete.

Screwtape then suggests a mind game that Wormwood should entice his patient to play: "Your patient must demand that all his own utterances are to be taken at their face value and judged simply on the actual words, while at the same time judging all his mother's utterances with the fullest and most over-sensitive interpretation of the tone and the context and the suspected intention. She must be encouraged to do the same to him. Hence from every quarrel they can both go away convinced, or very nearly convinced, that they are quite innocent." The insidiousness of this ploy is obvious, yet we have all succumbed to such temptation and therefore understand its efficacy.

The older devil then suggests how Wormwood can inflame all kinds of hostility in people, for once this habit is well established, he can actually encourage a human to say things "with the express purpose of offending and yet have a grievance when offense is taken." Clearly, this devil understands human psychology very well.

Sixth Letter

Screwtape addresses prayer in the fourth letter and also discusses the emotional states that spiritually hinder people. In the sixth letter he advises, "Do what you will, there is going to be some benevolence, as well as some malice, in your patient's soul. The great thing is to direct the malice to his immediate neighbors whom he meets every day and to thrust his benevolence out to the remote circumference, to people he does not know. The malice thus becomes wholly real and the benevolence largely imaginary."

Many people fall in love with humanity as a whole, as an idealized notion, yet remain very nasty to their neighbors. (Paul Johnson described this in his book *Intellectuals*, 1988.) Russian novelist Fyodor Dostoyevsky observed this same tendency in *The Brothers Karamazov*. One of his characters astutely observes this flaw within himself:

> But I marvel at myself: the more I love mankind in general, the less I love human beings in particular, separately, that is, as individual persons. In my dreams . . . I would often arrive at fervent plans of devotion to mankind and might very possibly have gone to the Cross for human beings, had that been suddenly required of me, and yet I am unable to spend two days in the same room with someone else. . . . No sooner is that someone else close to me than his personality crushes my self-esteem and hampers my freedom. In the space of a day and a night I am capable of coming to hate even the best of human beings: one because he takes too long over dinner, another because he has a cold and is perpetually blowing his nose. . . . It has always happened that the more I have hated human beings in particular, the more ardent has become my love for mankind in general. ([London: Penguin Classics, 2003], 79)

Even the popular sitcom *Seinfeld* noted this common sin dilemma when one of the characters proclaimed, "Humanity?

I love humanity! It's people I can't stand!" Ironically, we humans possess the ability to pride ourselves on our concern for the masses even when we spend our days abusing individuals. In contrast, Lewis wrote in an essay titled "The Weight of Glory,"

> The load, or weight, or burden of my neighbor's glory should be laid on my back, a load so heavy that only humility can carry it. . . . It is a serious thing . . . to remember that the dullest and most uninteresting person you can talk to may one day be a creature which, if you saw it now, you would be strongly tempted to worship, or else a horror and a corruption such as you now meet, if at all, only in a nightmare. All day long we are, in some degree, helping each other to one or other of these destinations. It is in the light of these overwhelming possibilities, it is with the awe and the circumspection proper to them, that we should conduct all our dealings with one another.

Sin would promote a selfishness that devalues others and destroys relationship, while God would have us enjoy the great privilege of loving each other properly and reaping the benefits of that love.

Screwtape also addresses the issue of whether the patient should be an extreme patriot or an extreme pacifist, given the nature of the war and his generalizations about humanity. His argument is that all extremes, except extreme devotion to the Enemy, are to be encouraged. Lewis's point is that Satan is indifferent as to which extreme we choose, for it is the imbalance, not the particular vice, that reduces our ability to live obediently and effectively.

Eighth Letter

Letter eight is one of my favorites. It contains a profound discussion about the laws of ups and downs, the troughs of life as well as its high points. Wormwood is convinced that it is a good thing that his patient is in a trough and depressed. Screwtape warns him against overconfidence. After all, it is often in the troughs of life that God can get people's best attention. Screwtape explains what he calls the law of Undulation—life is not steady; there are many ups and downs. There are times when God seems to be remarkably close to us, and there are also times of dryness. In some experiences God seems incredibly real and almost palpable, but other times the ceiling seems to be made of brass, preventing our prayers from leaving the room.

Through Screwtape, Lewis was describing something very significant here. He argues that "humans are amphibians—half spirit and half animal. (The Enemy's determination to produce such a revolting hybrid was one of the things that determined Our Father to withdraw his support from Him.) As spirits they belong to the eternal world, but as animals they inhabit time. This means that while their spirit can be directed to an eternal object, their bodies, passions, and imaginations are in continual change, for to be in time means to change."

He then introduces some important concepts. Screwtape explains, "To us a human is primarily food; our aim is the absorption of its will into ours, the increase of our own area of selfhood at its expense. But the obedience which the Enemy demands of men is quite a different thing. One must face the fact that all the talk about His love for men, and His service being perfect freedom, is not (as one would gladly believe) mere propaganda, but an appalling truth."

Now here is one of the most important lines in the entire book: "He really *does* want to fill the universe with a lot of loathsome little replicas of Himself—creatures whose life, on its miniature scale, will be qualitatively like His own, not because He has absorbed them but because their wills freely conform to His. We want cattle that can finally become food; He wants servants who can finally become sons."

It is at this point that Screwtape defines the essential difference between the Devil's goal and God's: "We want to suck in, He wants to give out. We are empty and would be filled; He is full and flows over. Our war aim is a world in which Our Father Below has drawn all other beings into himself: the Enemy wants a world full of beings united to Him but still distinct." Screwtape presents this grand mystery, and it is, in many ways, a depiction of the Creator and the creation, a reflection of the Trinitarian order in which there exists the I-thou relationship. We will always know the distinction between the Creator and the creation; yet, at the same time, there is a marvelous and mysterious union that we are being called to.

Even now the person in Christ can understand, or begin to glimpse, this marvelous mystery found in seven little words: *you in me and I in you*. Seven little words, sixteen little letters, express a mystery so profound that it cannot be fully understood this side of glory. The words *you in me* speak of our in-Christ relationship. We are positionally in Christ. The words *I in you* speak of Christ in us, and this refers to Christ empowering us for holy living. These are divine mysteries beyond explication, yet clearly, we are not consumed or absorbed, but rather, we become individuals who are beloved and who are also "one with Christ."

According to Screwtape, "the Irresistible and the Indisputable are the two weapons which the very nature of His scheme forbids Him to use." In other words, he is saying that God will not overwhelm or ravish us to the point where we have no choice but to submit.

> Merely to override a human will (as His felt presence in any but the faintest and most mitigated degree would certainly do) would be for Him useless. He cannot ravish. He can only woo. For His ignoble idea is to eat the cake and have it; the creatures are to be one with Him, but yet themselves; merely to cancel them, or assimilate them, will not serve. He is prepared to do a little overriding at the beginning. He will set them off with communications of His presence which, though faint, seem great to them, with emotional sweetness, and easy conquest over temptation.

Many times new believers enjoy a kind of honeymoon experience. It does seem that their prayers are answered in remarkable ways, and they often experience real victory over temptation. Yet Screwtape asserts that this does not remain the case permanently: "But He never allows this state of affairs to last long. Sooner or later He withdraws, if not in fact, at least from their conscious experience, all those supports and incentives. He leaves the creature to stand up on its own legs—to carry out from the will alone duties which have lost all relish."

Here Screwtape is alluding to God's maturing process for believers. Nature provides an apt metaphor. A mother eagle eventually wants her eaglets to learn to fly and leave the nest, so while they are young, she will begin removing some of the down from the nest, making it a little less comfortable each day. Then she takes the eaglets out of the nest, one by one, drops them in the air, swoops down to catch them before they fall too far, and returns them safely to the nest. This is an essential component of their flight training. This offers a wonderful analogy for what God does with us, as well (see Exodus 19:4; Deuteronomy 32:11). God removes some of our comforts in order to discipline and train us to walk by faith, not merely by sight. We must grow to love God for himself, and not just for his gifts.

Screwtape goes on to say, "It is during such trough periods, much more than during the peak periods, that it is growing into the sort of creature He wants it to be. Hence the prayers offered in the state of dryness are those which please Him best." This is a very important insight for us to keep in mind. As Lewis asserted in *Mere Christianity*, pain can serve as an effective megaphone to rouse deaf Christians.

Screwtape continues to teach Wormwood: "We can drag our patients along by continual tempting, because we design them only for the table, and the more their will is interfered with the better. He cannot 'tempt' to virtue as we do to vice.

He wants them to learn to walk and must therefore take away His hand." That is the idea. Just as parents must take away their hands and allow their children to stumble and get up to try again and again, similarly, God gently teaches us to walk by faith and in his power, not our own.

Perhaps my favorite passage from *The Screwtape Letters* is in chapter 8, where Screwtape observes, "And if only the will to walk is really there He is pleased even with their stumbles. Do not be deceived, Wormwood. Our cause is never more in danger than when a human, no longer desiring, but still intending, to do our Enemy's will, looks round upon a universe from which every trace of Him seems to have vanished, and asks why he has been forsaken, and still obeys." This is such a powerful statement. It is the conviction of Job in chapter 19 of that book, the certainty of Abraham in Genesis 22, and the confidence of Paul in 2 Timothy 4:17–18. I have read this sentence to several people during times of real troughs and despondency in their lives, and it has, in various ways, ministered to them. They have rediscovered dignity, in that God is giving them almost a backhanded compliment and letting them know that they need to walk by faith in the darkness. God is in them, is in front of and behind them, and is training them in the way of righteousness.

Ninth Letter

In letter nine there is a discussion about sensual temptations and pleasure, and I particularly appreciate one line from that letter: "Never forget that when we are dealing with any pleasure in its healthy and normal and satisfying form, we are, in a sense, on the Enemy's ground. I know we have won many a soul through pleasure. All the same, it is His invention, not ours. He made the pleasures: all our research so far has not enabled us to produce one."

This is a significant realization; all pleasure comes from God. As the senior demon admits, "All we can do is to encourage the humans to take the pleasures which our Enemy has produced, at times, or ways, or in degrees, which He has forbidden." Satan can try to distort God's good gifts and encourage us to enjoy them in the wrong way or at the wrong time, but Satan cannot create pleasure.

Psalm 16:11 states, "You will make known to me the path of life; in Your presence is fullness of joy; in Your right hand are pleasures forever." God is the wellspring of pleasure. However, I believe that God reduced our capacity to enjoy pleasure after the fall, and he also reduced our cognitive abilities, as well as our longevity. I believe these are all acts of grace because, as it is, we still live long enough and are smart enough to get ourselves into a heap of trouble. Imagine if a person had an IQ of 500 and could live one thousand years. What manner and level of evil might this person be able to accomplish? It is frightening, almost chilling, to consider.

I believe that the greatest pleasures we have ever known on earth are but trickles compared to the wellspring, the fountainhead of true pleasure that is God himself. We are not yet ready for the true pleasures of God's banquet table and his celestial city. Only when we are resurrected will we be able to appreciate those pleasures. However, he invites us to fidelity in this world, and even now he tells us that life is not so much about our happiness, but our holiness, and not so

much about our comfort, but our character.

In his book *The Problem of Pain*, Lewis showed us that it is as if Jesus were saying even now he will still give us great joys and life is going to be a gift. Lewis wrote, "Our Father refreshes us on the journey with some pleasant inns, but will not encourage us to mistake them for home" ([New York: HarperCollins, 2001], 116). So we press on, not expecting this world to be filled with all kinds of unremitting pleasure because we are not home yet. There are reminders, little hints of home, little pleasures we do have, but they are just hints of a greater joy we will share together.

Twelfth Letter

As you can see, each one of these letters concerns a different theme. While one letter contains some insights about humor—"Real humor and joy and fun are really things that we can't use very well. It is flippancy that we will use" to summarize Screwtape—others deal with daily life concerns and struggles. For instance, at the end of letter twelve, we find this description of the danger of succumbing to mediocrity:

> The Christians describe the Enemy as one "without whom Nothing is strong." And Nothing is very strong: strong enough to steal away a man's best years not in sweet sins but in a dreary flickering of the mind over it knows not what and knows not why, in the gratification of curiosities so feeble that the man is only half aware of them, in drumming of fingers and kicking of heels, in whistling tunes that he

does not like, or in the long, dim labyrinth of reveries that have not even lust or ambition to give them a relish, but which, once chance association has started them, the creature is too weak and fuddled to shake off.

Screwtape observes how distractions of the mundane dull our senses, diminish our pleasure, and encourage complacency. He goes on to say, "It does not matter how small the sins are provided that their cumulative effect is to edge the man away from the Light and out into the Nothing." So it does not matter how grand the sins seem; it only matters that we are edged further and further from the light and into a muddled nothingness or confusion. As Lewis's Screwtape observes, "Murder is no better than cards if cards can do the trick. Indeed the safest road to Hell is the gradual one—the gentle slope, soft underfoot, without sudden turnings, without milestones, without signposts."

Remaining Letters

There are several statements in the remaining letters that I think are potentially very helpful. In one section Screwtape is reminding his nephew about God and advises, "Remember always, that He really likes the little vermin," and here he is referring to human beings, "and sets an absurd value on the distinctness of every one of them. When He talks of their losing their selves, He only means abandoning the clamor of self-will; once they have done that, He really gives them back all their personality, and boasts (I am afraid, sincerely) that when they are wholly His they will be more themselves than ever." This is a fundamental theme in Christian theology. The fear of sinful humanity is loss of freedom, yet humanity was not created for autonomy. The great irony of the will is that it only works when it is submitted first to its Creator. The great gift of salvation is that in Christ we truly become ourselves. Satan would deceive us into believing just the opposite.

Later, in a letter on time, Lewis's demon argues that the past and the future bear little resemblance to eternity. In fact, the future bears the least resemblance to eternity. "The humans live in time but our Enemy destines them to eternity. He therefore, I believe, wants them to attend chiefly to two things, to eternity itself, and to that point of time which they call the Present. For the Present is the point at which time touches eternity." Here Lewis presented the idea that God desires for us to live in the present tense and relish the opportunities and the challenges of the present moment: "Of the present moment, and of it only, humans have an experience analogous to the experience which our Enemy has of reality as a whole." Satan would have us live in the regret or nostalgia of the past or the dread or anticipation of the future. God offers us the closest thing to eternity within time: life lived passionately in the present!

In speaking of the future, Screwtape notes, "In a word, the Future is, of all things, the thing *least like* eternity." He says, "He," speaking of the Enemy, "does not want men to give the Future their hearts, to place their treasure in it. We do." Many people give their hearts away for what is not and miss out on the opportunities of the present. It is possible, indeed very plausible, for many people to go through their lives always living in the ambitions and prospects of the future and never truly alive to the full challenges and relishing the opportunities and the giftedness of the present tense. When they realize that there is little time left, suddenly they revel nostalgically in the past and the good old days. In that way, they go through their whole lives never alive to the opportunities of the present tense—a great tragedy.

"We want a whole race," Screwtape says, "perpetually in pursuit of the rainbow's end, never honest, nor kind, nor happy *now*, but always using as mere fuel wherewith to heap the altar of the future every real gift which is offered to them in the Present." Satan aspires for us to waste the gift of the present and heap it on the altar of future prospects.

Moving on, the elder devil discusses gluttony in letter seventeen, but not a gluttony of excesses that you might suppose but rather "gluttony of Delicacy," where people can say they don't want much, just a little bit, properly done. These people give an appearance that they don't want much, but actually they want everything done according to their precise demands. This offers an interesting study on the idea of excess from a fresh perspective.

Letter eighteen addresses the idea of love and the implications of love as opposed to mere romantic sentiment. The nineteenth letter develops this a little more, and Screwtape admits that he can't understand the love of God: "All His talk about Love must be a disguise for something else. . . . The reason one comes to talk as if He really had this impossible Love is our utter failure to find out that real motive. What does He stand to make out of them? That is the insoluble question." The demons cannot understand sacrificial love because they are consumed with self. The idea of grace also offends the human consciousness because it is so different from the experiences of life and our own motivations. Therefore, we find ourselves suspicious of God's actions and motives.

Screwtape discusses helping a patient perceive misfortune as injury, and he also presents the "Miserific Vision," as opposed to the beatific vision: "He has filled His world full of pleasures," speaking here again of God. "There are things for humans to do all day long without His minding in the least—sleeping, washing, eating, drinking, making love, playing, praying, working. Everything has to be *twisted* before it's any use to us." The natural pleasures are areas that work for the tempter only when they are distorted.

In letter twenty-seven Screwtape talks about the importance of perspective. One of the things the demons want to do is to keep the patients away from a real perspective or to help them realize that "to regard the ancient writer as a possible source of knowledge—to anticipate that what he said could possibly modify your thoughts or your behavior—this would be rejected as unutterably simple-minded." In other words, they want people to be so parochial in their perspective that they absolutize the present tense. This is a characterization of our present culture. We lack historical depth and are concerned with only the social errors of the present. He goes on to say, "Since we cannot deceive the whole human race all the time, it is most important thus to cut every generation off from all others."

In other words, the demons do not want us to read old books because they provide fresh perspectives and ancient wisdom. "For where learning makes a free commerce between the ages there is always the danger that the characteristic errors of one may be corrected by the characteristic truths of another. But thanks be to Our Father and the Historical Point of View," as he calls it. "Great scholars are now as little nourished by the past as the most ignorant mechanic who holds that 'history is bunk.'"

One of Lewis's great peeves was that people are familiar with only what is current. The historical point of view is something that is regarded as being remote and irrelevant, and what we need is to solve our problems with only contemporary thinking and technology. After all, if it is new, it "must be better." He discussed this problem of intellectual snobbery at length in a book titled *The Discarded Image*.

In the twenty-eighth letter are some observations about prosperity. One of Wormwood's desires is to keep his patient alive because Wormwood has been failing in his endeavors. If he can move his patient toward his middle years, he may succumb to mediocrity or complacency, often characteristic of that phase of life. Screwtape affirms,

> If only he can be kept alive, you have time itself for your ally. The long, dull, monotonous years of middle-aged prosperity or middle-aged adversity are excellent campaigning weather. You see, it is so hard for these creatures to *persevere*. The routine of adversity, the gradual decay of youthful loves and youthful hopes, the quiet despair (hardly felt as pain) of ever overcoming the chronic temptations with which we have again and again defeated them, the drabness which we create in their lives and the inarticulate resentment with which we

teach them to respond to it—all this provides admirable opportunities of wearing out a soul by attrition. If, on the other hand, the middle years prove prosperous, our position is even stronger.

On the other hand, if a person is truly prosperous, as the world defines it, the devils can work with that as well: "Prosperity knits a man to the World. He feels that he is 'finding his place in it,' while really it is finding its place in him. His increasing reputation, his widening circle of acquaintances, his sense of importance, the growing pressure of absorbing and agreeable work, build up in him a sense of being really at home in earth which is just what we want." This, of course, is completely contrary to the biblical call to consider heaven as our true home and to live on earth as strangers and pilgrims (Philippians 3:20; 1 Peter 1:17).

In letter thirty Screwtape warns of the danger of commitment: "The thing to avoid is the total commitment. Whatever he *says*, let his inner resolution be not to bear whatever comes to him, but to bear it 'for a reasonable period'—and let the reasonable period be shorter than the trial is likely to last." Lewis's devils grasp that commitment and temptation are linked, for Screwtape goes on to say, "It need not be *much* shorter; in attacks on patience, chastity, and fortitude, the fun is to make the man yield just when (had he but known it) relief was almost in sight." This is a theme that we find in Scripture as well. Humans yield too soon. If only we would persevere. God has said that Christ's holiness is sufficient to overcome our weaknesses (2 Corinthians 12:7–10).

Finally, in the last letter, it turns out that all is lost; Wormwood's patient escapes his grasp. Screwtape angrily declares, "You have let a soul slip through your fingers." The patient has died, and in his death he has seen a vision. First, he sees Wormwood, and he realizes that he was the one tempting him. Then he sees angels, and he realizes that they were encouraging him along the way.

Screwtape tells Wormwood, "I know how it was. You reeled back dizzy and blinded, more hurt by them [angels] than he had ever been by bombs. The degradation of it!— that this thing of earth and slime could stand upright and converse with spirits before whom you, a spirit, could only cower." He goes on to say, "He had no faintest conception till that very hour of how they would look, and even doubted their existence. But when he saw them he knew that he had always known them and realized what part each one of them had played at many an hour in his life when he had supposed himself alone, so that now he could say to them, one by one, not, 'Who *are* you?' but 'So it was *you* all the time.'"

I wonder if that will be true for us when we die. Again, Lewis was only speculating, but perhaps when we are before the Lord, we will realize the incredible work and warfare that were around us. Remember what it says in Hebrews about the angels? "Are not all angels ministering spirits sent to serve those who will inherit salvation?" (Hebrews 1:14 NIV). This means that powerful angels of God—which, if we saw them, we would be overwhelmed—actually are our servants sent by God to minister to us in our mundane lives. This is an incredible thought and should help us see our daily lives as extraordinary.

A Taste of the Classics

My conviction is that we will finally know some day what role angels played in our lives. On several occasions I suspected their presence. Two instances, particularly, come to mind, and both occurred while I was driving. In each case, something told me not to go forward. Once I was going to make a left turn, and there was a Volvo station wagon in front of me when the light turned green. The Volvo made a left turn to head north. I was going to do the same, but something kept me from going on; I don't know what it was. I don't normally wait like that. In that moment of pause, a car sped through the red light. Had I followed that Volvo, assuming that it was safe to go, I would have been crushed. In that moment I immediately felt an angelic presence.

Something very similar happened about a year ago. Again, it was a situation where something prompted me not to proceed through an intersection when another car sped through the red light. We do not know what is going on around us in the unseen realms, but I hope that some day we will be able to glorify the Lord even more to learn of all the ministrations that occured to help us on our way.

At the end of the book, Screwtape says, "He [the patient] saw not only Them; he saw Him," speaking about the Lord. "This animal, this thing begotten in a bed, could look on Him. What is blinding, suffocating fire to you, is now cool light to him, is clarity itself, and wears the form of a Man." Isn't that a beautiful picture? He could see the resurrected Christ and stand before him with confidence. Screwtape then observes to Wormwood, "All the delights of sense, or heart, or intellect, with which you could once have tempted him, even the delights of virtue itself, now seem to him in

[32]

comparison but as the half nauseous attractions of a raddled harlot would seem to a man who hears that his true beloved whom he has loved all his life and whom he had believed to be dead is alive and even now at his door."

This is the truth we must, by grace, strive to keep in mind—the insipidity of these temptations. How weak they are! How foolish they are when we see them in their true light. Screwtape then describes the glory of being in God's presence:

> He is caught up into that world where pain and pleasure take on transfinite values and all our arithmetic is dismayed. Once more, the inexplicable meets us. Next to the curse of useless tempters like yourself the greatest curse upon us is the failure of our Intelligence Department. If only we could find out what He is really up to! Alas, alas, that knowledge, in itself so hateful and mawkish a thing, should yet be necessary for Power! Sometimes I am almost in despair. All that sustains me is the conviction that our Realism, our rejection (in the face of all temptations) of all silly nonsense and claptrap, *must* win in the end. Meanwhile, I have you to settle with. Most truly do I sign myself . . .

Ironically, throughout the book, Screwtape has signed all his letters "Your affectionate uncle Screwtape." Now, at the very end of the book in the very last letter, he ominously signs it "Your increasingly and ravenously affectionate uncle Screwtape." Wormwood has failed in his mission, so

Screwtape is going to devour him into himself. The affection is actually a ravenous appetite for self-gratification, not love.

Throughout this work, Lewis created powerful images through opposites and irony and reversals. Lewis provided the reader with sound theology, yet through a surprising lens. Ordinary daily life turns out to be truly extraordinary when seen from the viewpoint of devilish warfare waged against us. One of Lewis's great skills was his ability to use words to open readers' eyes to truth.

Lord, we thank you for this marvelous book. May we be people who walk with dignity and with prudence. Guard our feet, our steps, our directions, and our choices, knowing that these are the "stuff" of which eternity is made. May we be a people of fidelity, of hope, and of purpose, realizing that the things to which you call us are more than worth whatever sacrifices we make here. We pray in Jesus' name. Amen.

NOTES

NOTES

Paradise Lost

Introduction

Literary scholars generally acknowledge Milton to be one of the greatest English poets, second only to Shakespeare. Of all his works, *Paradise Lost* is regarded as his supreme achievement and the greatest epic poem of the English language. It is a massive composition written in the classic style that was inherited from the Greeks and Romans. It concerns the biblical story of the fall of Adam and Eve and elaborately describes the cosmic events surrounding this narrative through extraordinary movements from the heights of heaven to the depths of hell. *Paradise Lost* systematically explores the vast corpus of theology and does so in an animated, exciting, and imaginative way. I am stunned by the depths of Milton's literary imagination that allowed him to take ideas from Scripture and weave them into a colorful, intricate, and yet substantial narrative fabric.

Milton is regarded by many as the most learned of the English authors. Certainly, he studied intensely and drank deeply at the well of classic writings while studying Greek, Latin, and Hebrew. Along with his scholarly grasp of ancient literature and history, Milton possessed a tremendous ability to coherently mix allusions from the Bible, medieval angelology, ancient Jewish tradition, apocryphal accounts, and classical mythology. As a result, there is something for everyone in Milton's works. Musicians, theologians, educators, historians, and those from many other fields of study have written widely about Milton, appreciating his vast impact.

Biographical Sketch

Milton's life can be viewed in three periods. The first period, from 1608 to 1639, marked his early life. The second period, from 1640 to 1659, proved to be a time of great emotional tumult for him. The third period, from 1660 to 1674, encompassed his final years.

Early Life (1608–1639)

John Milton was born in London and spent his first years there. His father's prosperity afforded him private tutoring and an early knowledge of Greek and Latin. Later he also acquired proficiency in French, Spanish, Italian, Old English, and Dutch. He graduated from Christ's College, Cambridge, in 1625 and remained there to earn a master of arts degree in 1632. At Cambridge he gained a reputation for skill in poetry.

Following this formal education, he retired to his family's country home and engaged in further intensive private study for six years. This opportunity offered him enough privacy to focus on his poetry and literary pursuits, as well as explore a wide range of study. In 1637 and 1638 he traveled widely in France and Italy, moving in some of the most intellectual and influential social circles. Through these connections Milton was able to discuss the issues of the day with such notables as Galileo as well as patrons of the arts and Catholic cardinals. It was also during this period that he wrote his lyric poems and sonnets. I would say that the human side of Milton is visible most clearly in these early writings, which, by the way, employ complex rhyming structures.

Middle Years (1640–1659)

Milton returned to England during a politically turbulent period. An armed conflict between King Charles I and his parliamentary opponents was imminent. Milton, who was a Puritan, sided with the parliamentary cause, writing many articles in which he passionately argued his political, social, and religious ideas. One of his polemics, entitled *Areopagitica*, concerned the right to publish ideas for public discussion and is considered a classic essay on the freedom of the press. During the two civil war years, he became very much involved with Oliver Cromwell and ultimately became Latin secretary to Cromwell in 1649. In this office Milton composed the foreign correspondence and propaganda for the Commonwealth of England.

With the death of Cromwell in 1658, the English republic began to collapse into feuding factions. Milton clung to his antiroyalist and antiepiscopal beliefs and continued to publish political and religious articles. He was very strongly a republican and was opposed to any form of a state-established church with a priesthood paid by the state. The majority of his writings from this period were highly politicized and formal.

As evident in his writings during this twenty-year period, Milton never resolved the tensions he felt between liberty and discipline, passion and reason, human love and the providence of God, nor did he resolve the conflict between the necessity for individualism and the need for a social construct. Some writings show him to be religiously nonorthodox. For example, he misunderstood the doctrine of the Trinity because he believed the Son to be subordinate to the Father.

During this turbulent political period, Milton suffered personal turmoil as well. He experienced a number of physical ailments and gradually went blind, losing his sight completely by age forty-four. So while still serving as the Latin secretary, he was totally dependent on others to help him fulfill his duties. Some years later he composed "Sonnet 19," a powerful poem that conveys his despair as he struggled to come to terms with his blindness. In it he questioned how he could still be expected to serve God effectively while being denied his sight. In the midst of his anguish, he realized that

God needed neither his talents nor his effort, triumphantly asserting, "They also serve who only stand and wait." This is a beautiful expression of a biblical truth that we tend to forget. We don't actually live *for* God; we live *in* Christ. The apostle Paul clarified this when he wrote in Galatians 2:20, "I have been crucified with Christ and I no longer live, but Christ lives in me. The life I live in the body, I live by faith in the Son of God, who loved me and gave himself for me" (NIV). Although as Christians we do aspire to live our lives for God's glory, God does not need or demand our service; as Milton rightly understood, God demands our very lives. He delights in *us*, not in our productivity. I think this is perhaps Milton's finest sonnet.

Final Years (1660-1674)

In 1660 the monarchy was restored, and Milton was forced into hiding when a warrant was issued for his arrest and for his writings to be burned. Milton reemerged when, because of influential friends, a pardon was issued. With his hopes for political and religious reformation completely dashed and with the loss of his position, much of his wealth, and his eyesight, he retired to a quiet, personal life in London and focused on composing major poems. In 1663 Milton married for a third time—his first two wives died following complications of childbirth. Three of Milton's five children lived to adulthood, but his relationship with them was strained. His writings during his final years reveal a mature perspective.

Paradise Lost was published in 1667; a second epic, *Paradise Regained*, and a third, *Samson Agonistes*, were published together in 1671. *Paradise Regained* is not up to the level of *Paradise Lost*, but *Samson Agonistes* is a remarkable achievement. In all these works Milton was dealing with the personal despair of his political disappointment, and yet he affirmed human potential. Perhaps, it was this profound disappointment that was crucial for the development of his depth of insight, and it may have transferred his hopes from political machinations to the eternal verities.

Epic poems of this quality can only be completed at a stage in life when a person possesses both extensive knowledge and poetic skills. The best evidence of this is that both Homer and Virgil wrote their epic masterpieces near the ends of their lives, as did Dante. Each of these authors had acquired a perspective that could be gained only through difficulties and pain over a number of years, something surely Milton shared with them. Apparently, Milton birthed the concept for *Paradise Lost* in 1640, but it would be twenty-seven years before he would actually create it. This may have produced a tension in his life—one that many poets feel—between an impulse to complete his poem and another to refrain from finishing it until his ideas had ripened sufficiently.

Milton endured the added tensions of frustrated political dreams and blindness, but perhaps it was these very limitations that eventually supplied him—as deafness to Beethoven—a preternatural concentration that enabled him to write of heaven and hell and the pre-fall world on his own terms. Finally, he could see clearly with his mind's eye. Finally, he could devote himself to this focus. Finally, he could use his vast wealth of knowledge and produce something unique—an epic poem that would tell the whole human story from the beginning to the end.

The dramatic scope of *Paradise Lost* required a great mind, a vast perspective, and much suffering. The nineteenth-century English poet Samuel Taylor Coleridge characterized Milton this way: "Finding it impossible to realize his own aspirations, either in religion, or politics, or society, he gave up his heart to the living spirit and light within him, and avenged himself on the world by enriching it with this record of his own transcendent ideal" (Paul Hamilton, *Coleridge's Poetics* [Palo Alto, CA: Stanford University Press, 1983], 139). Indeed, he did avenge himself because he left this legacy. We would likely know little about the other periods of his life were it not for this enduring work.

Style

The grand style of *Paradise Lost* reveals an attempt by Milton to do for England what Homer had done for the Greeks and Virgil for the Romans—that is, create his nation's greatest epic poem. His narrative style reflects certain elements that both those authors employed. Epic poems tell ancient stories and celebrate great national heroes. In the case of *Paradise Lost*, Christ is the hero while Adam and Eve serve as hero-protagonists. Also included in an epic is a central feat acted out within a cosmic scope that has a supernatural dimension. In the writings of Homer and Virgil, the mythological gods were at work behind the scenes, but Milton Christianized those elements and replaced the gods with the true God and his angelic hosts.

Indeed, we might even regard this work as not so much an epic but an anti-epic, because the human heroes turn out to be archetypal sinners, and their epic feat is a fall from innocence. The crucial struggle of this story does not take place on a battlefield, as in the *Iliad*, but rather it takes place in the human soul. The great conquest consists not in military action, but rather it is reflected in repentance and salvation and obedience to the living God. The fall from innocence creates the desperate condition and the cosmic struggle of the story and also illustrates the human condition we still find ourselves in today.

I think that the power and the charm of the great poets of antiquity are best revealed to us as we read Milton. We can experience the power of their ancient style without needing a translation; we have something that is immediately accessible to us. I like what Samuel Johnson said in 1783, when referring to *Paradise Lost*, "Poetry is the art of uniting pleasure with truth, by calling imagination to the help of reason" (*Lives of the English Poets, Volume 1* [Elibron Classics series, 2006], 104). This is a very profound observation. The passion and feelings of literary imagination invite our reason to go beyond itself, much like music helps us transcend the mere text of a hymn. Our emotions are evoked, and this can invite us to a deeper state of worship.

In characterizing this magnificent work, Johnson further commented, "The subject . . . of Milton is not the destruction of a city, the conduct of a colony, or the foundation of an empire. His subject is the fate of worlds, the revolutions of heaven and earth; rebellion against the supreme King, raised by the highest order of created beings; the overthrow of their host, and the punishment of their crime; the creation of a new race of reasonable creatures; their original happiness and innocence, their forfeiture of immortality, and their restoration to hope and peace" (105). What an excellent summary of the themes of this book.

As we discuss these motifs, we will see that *Paradise Lost* incorporates intensely spiritual and biblically driven images. It is a sublime poem characterized by what we might call an expansive loftiness. In fact, I think Milton possessed a particular power to astonish. He was able to take the narrative of the first three chapters of Genesis and plausibly embellish it to provide the reader a credible picture of the Edenic paradise. His art gives us an almost palpable experience of the spiritual warfare between God's holy angels and Satan's demons. Milton takes us into the demonic abyss, into their chaos, and into their councils in Pandemonium—the capital of hell in Milton's tale. The word *pandemonium* originated from this work. Milton combined two Greek words, *pan*, which means "all," and *daimonion*, which means "lesser god" or "demon." There they hold their councils and scheme their revenge.

Paradise Lost moves the reader through the vast fabric of Christian doctrine, not merely to inform but also to contrast the good life God planned for us at creation with what that life has become through the tragedy of sin. Writing again of Milton, Johnson observed, "Milton's delight was to sport in the wide regions of possibility; reality was a scene too narrow for his mind. He sent his faculties out upon discovery, into worlds where only imagination can travel, and delighted to form new modes of existence, and furnish sentiment and action to superior beings, to trace the counsels of hell, or accompany the choirs of heaven" (109). The literary theorist Northrop Frye said it well when he wrote, "Every student of Milton has been rewarded according to his efforts and his ability. The only ones who have abjectly failed with him are those who have tried to cut him down to size—their size" (Northrop Frye and Angela Esterhammer, *Northrop Frye on Milton and Blake* [Toronto: University of Toronto Press, 2005], 36–37).

C. S. Lewis also contended that Milton's great work has been frequently misunderstood by modern literary theorists and readers. He explained this by observing that ancient and medieval epics had presented plots that were essentially perennial; their conflicts, while temporarily resolved, were doomed to be repeated. He then went on to observe, "But *Paradise Lost* records a real, irreversible, unrepeatable process in the history of the universe; and even for those who do not believe this, it embodies (in what *for them* is mythical form) the great change in every individual soul from happy dependence to miserable self-assertion and thence either, as in Satan, to final isolation, or, as in Adam, to reconcilement and a different happiness." He continued, "After Blake, Milton criticism is lost in misunderstanding, and the true line is hardly found again until Mr. Charles Williams's preface" (*A Preface to Paradise Lost* [New York: Oxford University Press, 1961], 133). Lewis truly grasped the purpose of this marvelous work. Some critics actually "may hate Milton," Lewis wrote, "through fear and envy. . . . It is not rustic, [naïve], or unbuttoned. It will therefore be unintelligible to those who lack the right qualifications, and hateful to the baser spirits among them. *Paradise Lost* has been compared to the great wall of China, and the comparison is good: both are among the wonders of the world and both divide the tilled fields and cities of an ancient culture from the barbarians. We have only to add that the wall is necessarily hated by those who see it from the wrong side, and the parallel is complete" (135). Lewis did not make himself popular with many critics with these words, yet his assertions are insightful.

Survey

Paradise Lost was originally published in 1667 in ten books; a later version in 1674 divided the work into twelve books. These books were intentionally aligned into couplets of six books each that provide us with a movement of contrasting flows, like the movements of a symphony. Books 1 and 2 provide images of hell. The angelic fall has already taken place, and Satan and his forces are experiencing defeat and pain and suffering. They are full of revenge, hatred, futility, and delusion because their heavenly rebellion was crushed by the remaining angelic forces and the Son of God, about whom we read later in this epic.

The first two books were written in what some literary critics have termed the *demonic style*, as opposed to a *celestial style*. This demonic style is very baroque, which means that it is ornate, flashy, highly involved, dense, and weighed down with allusions to classical mythology. It is difficult to follow even for the reader who is familiar with mythology. This style itself illustrates the pandemonium, the confusion, the chaos, and the discordant wills that are represented in the councils of Satan.

In the next two books, the writing changes to the celestial style, which, by comparison, is simple, elegant, and light, easier to follow, and filled with allusions to Scripture. Familiarity with the Bible makes these chapters less demanding than the first two. Book 3 introduces the reader to the imagery of heaven, and book 4 relates the story of the garden of Eden. Book 4 is an astounding achievement and is my favorite part. It is characterized by a lucidity, a lightness, a clarity, and a beauty that I think Milton deliberately used to illustrate the corresponding qualities of the spiritual realms. So, in the first four books there is a movement from hell to heaven and, finally, to paradise on earth.

Books 5 and 6 depict the angelic war in heaven, followed by the eviction of Satan and his forces. This is one of the most exciting battle scenes imaginable. It is an epic contest that, if not for Milton's thematic purpose, could stand alone as a great war story. In books 7 and 8, Milton moves the reader to the contrasting event of creation. After the destructive effects of the satanic rebellion in heaven, we witness the beautiful drama of the creation of the heavens and earth. In this sense, the reader participates in the rhythmic movement from the horrific to the sublime.

Books 9 and 10 chronicle the fall of Adam and Eve and its effects. We are brought vividly into that crisis, that climax, that event that we have read about repeatedly. We know what is to happen, and yet somehow Milton creates a tension and a dread that cause us to almost believe that Adam and Eve will resist the temptation. We see the garden of Eden illuminated, allowing us a fresh access to the scene. (This is not unlike, though different in a sense, what Lewis did in The Chronicles of Narnia. He presented the gospel in a fresh and new way for children's eyes.) We see what we already know, yet we feel what we had not felt before.

Especially in book 10 we are reminded that the fall did not happen accidentally. The fall was an intentional choice of disobedience. Likewise, every sin is a kind of fall, a movement away from relationship with God. The imagery here causes us to question how we would behave in similar circumstances.

The final two books, which I regard as the least successful of this work, include a vision of future events. Here the fall of humanity is balanced by restoration, grief is balanced by consolation, and pessimism is mitigated by hope. Book 11 retells the biblical story from the fall to the flood, and book 12 tells of Abraham to the second coming of Christ. Milton intricately wove all the threads of Scripture together to present the story of God's redemption of humanity through a rich tapestry of extraordinary imagery.

Milton's work is difficult to read because he wrote in such a lofty style, employing very long sentences and an extensive vocabulary. However, Paradise Lost is a unified poem. There is not a single line or sentence that is not connected to preceding material; everything works backward and forward in a fluidity of syntax and significance.

I think much of the power of *Paradise Lost* is found in what has been called its great argument, that is, its architecture of themes and ideas. The moral and spiritual conflict between good and evil is the most obvious. It presents a Christian view of history, which unfolds as a sequence and emphasizes a hierarchy that, in Milton's age, was portrayed as a great chain of being, with reason as a means to virtue when it is achieved by governing the emotions and the appetites, thereby moving us forward toward God's reasonable commands. Milton clearly presents evil as disobedience to God. I find that this book appeals to and touches the emotions. Milton achieved this by guiding his readers to vicariously imagine themselves in the events and tensions of the epic. This, I think, is significant because it allows the story to become personal and experiential and to touch us on a deeper level in that regard.

Milton felt it necessary to defend his style of blank verse because at this time people believed that poems should be written exclusively in rhyme. Milton wrote this comment before his text, "The measure is English heroic verse without rhyme, as that of Homer in Greek, and of Virgil in Latin; rhyme being no necessary adjunct or true ornament of poem or good verse, in longer works especially, but the invention of a barbarous age, to set off wretched matter and lame meter." He went on to say, "This neglect then of rhyme so little is to be taken for a defect, though it may seem so perhaps to vulgar readers, that it rather is to be esteemed an example set, the first in English, of ancient liberty recovered to heroic poem from the troublesome and modern bondage of rhyming." Critics of the day, however, were not pleased.

Book 1

At the beginning of each book, Milton provided an outline for that particular argument. The argument of book 1 is that at the command of God, Satan and his demons are driven out of heaven, after which they fall into chaos. We see Satan and his demons submerged in a burning lake. Satan is "thunderstruck and astonished, after a certain space recovers, as from confusion, calls up him who next in order and dignity lay by him; they confer of their miserable fall. Satan awakens all his legions, who lay till then in the same manner confounded; they rise, their numbers, array of battle, their chief leaders named, according to the idols known afterwards in Canaan and the countries adjoining."

Satan places the demons behind the gods and goddesses of the Canaanites, the Assyrians, and the Babylonians. This illustrates the spiritual forces behind the political machinations of the nations. The passage continues, "To these Satan directs his speech, comforts them with hope yet of regaining heaven, but tells them lastly of a new world and new kind of creature to be created, according to an ancient prophecy or report in heaven; for that angels were long before this visible creation, was the opinion of many ancient Fathers. To find out the truth of this prophecy, and what to determine thereon he refers to a full council. What his associates thence attempt. Pandaemonium the palace of Satan rises, suddenly built out of the deep: the infernal peers there sit in council." There is a direct irony here, for in Greek mythology, Chaos, the disordered entity existent before creation, somehow spawned love and light and the rest of creation. Here in Milton's text, Pandemonium is the futile attempt to create and build in defiance of God, and it is revealed for the atrocity that it really is.

The first invocation of the poem reads, "Of man's first disobedience, and the fruit of that forbidden tree, whose mortal taste brought death into the world, and all our woe, with loss of Eden, till one greater man restore us, and regain the blissful seat, sing heavenly muse, that on the secret top of Oreb, or of Sinai, didst inspire that shepherd, who first taught the chosen seed, in the beginning how the heavens and earth rose out of chaos." Milton here reminded us that Moses, on Mount Sinai, was inspired to reveal the truth to God's people. Milton referred here to a muse, but his was not one of the muses of the Greeks. Many of the ancient epics, including those of Homer, appealed to muses for their inspiration. However, Milton's muse "wast present, and with mighty wings outspread dove-like sat'st brooding on the vast abyss." So, he was appealing to the Holy Spirit. He continued, "And mad'st it pregnant: what in me is dark illumine, what is low raise and support; that to the height of this great argument I may assert eternal providence, and justify the ways of God to men." This was his intention for *Paradise Lost*: to assert the weight of "eternal providence" and make it an apologetic to "justify the ways of God to men."

Later on in book 1, Satan reflects, "The mind is its own place, and in itself can make a heaven of hell, a hell of heaven." He goes on, "Here we may remain secure, and in my choice to reign is worth ambition though in hell: better to reign in hell, than serve in heaven." As Satan utters this defiant statement, he is helplessly bobbing about in agony in the lake of fire, and like Dante's frozen and impotent Satan in *Inferno*, in an ironic attempt to assert the will, Satan imprisons and destroys himself. This is the essence of the satanic plot. This is the image of futility. This is the consequence of the usurpation of the will.

Also in book 1 there is an allusion that in God's "regal state put forth at full, but still his strength concealed, which tempted our attempt, and wrought our fall." Here Satan alludes to an idea that I actually hold myself—that Satan's forces completely failed to comprehend the awesome power of the living God. Despite what they had witnessed in heaven, there must have been some concealment; otherwise, it seems impossible for them to have supposed that they could become God's equals. Dostoyevsky once asserted that God took his greatest risk in bestowing free will on his creatures. And for the will to be a real, no-strings-attached gift, it must be able to defy as well as to submit. The horrible mystery of evil is how those who were once rational and relational could volitionally choose, to their eternal misery, to embrace irrationality and alienation.

Book 2

In book 2 various demons are speaking in their councils. One named Moloch says in effect, "What shall we do? Shall we just keep sitting here?" Here he appeals to plain rage, for he is not the brightest of these fallen beings; he is very simple minded, a mere rat in a trap. Belial, in his council, says, "What can we suffer worse? Is this then worst, thus sitting, thus consulting, thus in arms? What when we fled amain, pursued and struck with heaven's afflicting thunder . . . ?" He espouses the opposite opinion of Moloch. He advocates keeping a quiet profile because things could be worse. The etymology of the word *mammon* comes from a pagan god of wealth, and so the demon bearing that name suggests that with skill and art they could turn their abode into a heaven of their own and simply "blind" themselves "to the necessary discrepancies." This is a frightening thought, and I fear many people in our own time have fallen prey to this delusion. In fact, it is the seductive lie of existential philosophy that we can, of our own making, enjoy a self-made heaven on earth in lieu of the real one. The voice of Beelzebub is then heard, and he gives the wisest counsel. He brings them back to reality by saying, "This place our dungeon, not our safe retreat." They finally grasp that they can neither escape nor hurt their enemy, but perhaps there is a chance of injuring someone else. Thus, Beelzebub comes up with this counsel: "Seduce them to our party, that their God may prove their foe, and with repenting hand abolish his own works. This would surpass common revenge, and interrupt his joy in our confusion, and our joy upraise in his disturbance; when his darling sons hurled headlong to partake with us, shall curse their frail original, and faded bliss, faded so soon." So, Beelzebub suggests that they not merely sit there "hatching vain empires." He argues that they seduce the one who is about to be created, and the councils agree.

I believe that Satan is the most convincing of Milton's characters. I would suggest that Lewis was right on the mark when he suggested,

In all but a few writers the 'good' characters are the least successful, and every one who has ever tried to make even the humblest story ought to know why. To make a character worse than oneself it is only necessary to release imaginatively from control some of the bad passions which, in real life, are always straining at the leash . . . the moment the leash is slipped, to come out and have in our books that holiday we try to deny them in our lives. But if you try to draw a character better than yourself, all you can do is . . . to imagine them prolonged and more consistently embodied in action. We do not really know what it feels like to be a man much better than ourselves. . . . The Satan in Milton enables him to draw the character well just as the Satan in us enables us to receive it. (*A Preface to Paradise Lost*, 100–101)

Those are frightening words, indeed. The reality here is that our minds are deficient and that is why we always read Dante's *Inferno* and don't generally enjoy his *Paradiso* as much—it is not as convincing. It is harder to write about good, and make it convincing, than it is to write of evil. It is a struggle that any good writer understands.

Books 3 and 4

In book 3 we first observe the heavenly scene, followed by the creation of the Paradise on earth. God, foreseeing the fall that is to occur, even before the creation of human beings, reveals his solution to their hellish hate: Christ. He declares, "Their own both righteous and unrighteous deeds, and live in thee transplanted, and from thee receive new life. So man, as is most just, shall satisfy for man, be judged and die, and dying rise, and rising with him raise his brethren, ransomed with his own dear life. So heavenly love shall outdo hellish hate." God's ultimate solution is that his Son will present himself as the perfect substitute for humanity and accomplish what no creature could accomplish—the subjugation of the will. Thus heavenly love will outdo hellish hate.

Book 4 establishes the tension as Satan conversely declares, "So farewell hope, and with hope farewell fear, farewell remorse: all good to me is lost; evil be thou my good; by thee at least divided empire with heaven's king I hold by thee, and more than half perhaps will reign; as man ere long, and this new world shall know." We see him before the act of seducing, saying that evil will become his good and that he seeks to be as destructive as possible. While there is a clear contrast presented here between good and evil, it is not a dualistic dichotomy. Even here, early in the epic, it is obvious that evil cannot succeed on any enduring scale; Satan knows he is beaten, and the reader recognizes rebellion's impotence and God's sovereignty.

Book 4 also relates the creation of Eve. She is apart from Adam and has not yet seen him but glimpses herself reflected in water:

> I thither went with unexperienced thought,
> and laid me down on the green bank, to look

into the clear smooth lake, that to me seemed another sky. As I bent down to look, just opposite, a shape within the watery gleam appeared bending to look on me, I started back, it started back, but pleased I soon returned, pleased it returned as soon with answering looks of sympathy and love; there I had fixed mine eyes till now, and pined with vain desire, had not a voice thus warned me, What thou seest, what there thou seest fair creature is thyself, with thee it came and goes: but follow me, and I will bring thee where no shadow stays thy coming, and thy soft embraces, he whose image thou art, him thou shall enjoy inseparably thine, to him shalt bear multitudes like thyself, and thence be called mother of human race: what could I do, but follow straight, invisibly thus led?

What marvelous, sublime imagery, including that of plant life, animals, harmony, and even of sexual union as well. Milton viewed the amorous embraces here as in a prelapsarian condition, that is, before the fall. This is something that he celebrated in this section. God is the one who gives the great gift of life and the next most important gift— the awesome freedom that permeates his creation. Milton thought that God's greatest gift to man was reason and the freedom to exercise that reason in the act of choosing. A man incapable of making a mistake would have been a man incapable of significant decisions, incapable of enjoying a sense of achievement, and incapable of the God-like pleasure of freely making a gift, as in the joy of giving thanks. Such a man incapable of true obedience to God would have no human dignity or worth, as Milton defined those terms.

I am truly struck that even Voltaire appreciated the God of Milton, in contrast to his own representation of God as an infinitely powerful tyrant. He wrote, "The God of *Milton* is always a Creator, a Father, and a Judge; nor is his Vengeance jarring with his Mercy, nor his Predeterminations repugnant to the Liberty of Man. These are the Pictures which lift up, indeed, the Soul of the Reader" (Voltaire and Nicholas Cronk, *Letters Concerning the English Nation* [New York: Oxford University Press, 1994], 154–5). Voltaire's observations are a tribute to Milton's biblical depiction of God's character.

Books 5 and 6

In book 5 we witness the destructive forces of evil as we hear the story of the rebellion within the angelic order. This order will later influence human action, both positively and negatively. Milton painted a portrait of war in heaven. The obedient angelic forces remain faithful to God and form a community of service led by four key angels. Gabriel provides a ministry of responsibility, Raphael provides instruction, Michael provides command, and Uriel provides vigilance. Five other obedient angels are also named, though only two are named in Scripture; two others are mentioned in apocryphal literature.

One of the pivotal quotes from this book is when Raphael is speaking to Adam: "Son of heaven and earth, attend: that thou art happy, owe to God; that thou continuest such, owe to thyself." Raphael is warning him to be aware that a fiend is on the loose, so that he won't succumb to the temptation. Raphael goes on to say, "That is, to thy obedience; therein stand. This was that caution given thee; be advised. God made thee perfect, not immutable; and good he made thee, but to persevere he left it in thy power, ordained thy will by nature free, not overruled by fate inextricable, or strict necessity; our voluntary service he requires."

Moving on to book 6, in the heavenly battle, Satan is pierced through by a lance from the archangel Michael: "The sword of Michael from the armory of God was given him tempered so, that neither keen nor solid might resist that edge: it met the sword of Satan with steep force to smite descending, and in half cut sheer, nor stayed, but with swift wheel reverse, deep entering sheared all his right side; then Satan first knew pain, and writhed him to and fro convolved; so sore the grinding sword with discontinuous wound passed through him, but the ethereal substance closed not long divisible, and from the gash a stream of nectarous humor issuing flowed sanguine, such as celestial spirits may bleed."

According to Milton's imagery, his angels do not consist of the four elements commonly believed by the medieval world to compose matter: earth, air, fire, and water. Rather, to them is attributed a unique quality—a "quintessence." This denotation means "fifth essence." Unable to explain the uniqueness of humanity in relation to the rest of creation, the medievalist attributed the differences to a fifth element that must be distinct to it alone. Ether was a relatively new discovery, and so it became the symbol of that distinction, or "soulness," and it is from that same word we get the word *ethereal*. In keeping with this assumption, Milton's angels are composed of an ethereal substance. They cannot be fatally wounded because this mysterious substance allows them to immediately heal. The tremendous angelic warfare, which includes heaving mountains back and forth, is finally brought to an end when the Son of God comes on the third day and hurls the demonic forces into the abyss.

Books 7 and 8

As we move into book 7, we witness Milton's beautiful juxtaposition of the destructive wicked forces with God's divine creativity. We see Milton's description that was built on creation accounts in Scripture and also on the mass of commentary of those accounts. An angel informs Adam that all things were brought into being by God, and he reports, "And of the sixth day yet remained; there wanted yet the masterwork, the end of all yet done; a creature who not prone and brute as other creatures, but endued with sanctity of reason, might erect his stature, and upright with front serene govern the rest, self-knowing, and from thence magnanimous to correspond with heaven, but grateful to acknowledge whence his good descends, thither with heart and voice and eyes directed in devotion, to adore and worship God supreme, who made him chief of all his works." This is beautiful and rich imagery depicting the creation of Adam. At the end of book 8, the reader is reminded that humans are called, not to be constrained, but to obey and to choose a willingness to serve the living God, "whom to love is to obey."

Book 9

In book 9, in the opening argument, we discover

> Satan having compassed the earth, with meditated guile returns as a mist by night into Paradise, enters into the serpent sleeping. Adam and Eve, in the morning go forth to their labors, which Eve proposes to divide in several places, each laboring apart: Adam consents not, alleging the danger, lest that enemy, of whom they were forewarned, should attempt her found alone. Eve loath to be thought not circumspect or firm enough, urges her going apart, the rather desirous to make trial of her strength; Adam at last yields: the serpent finds her alone; his subtle approach, first gazing, then speaking, with much flattery extolling Eve above all other creatures. Eve wondering to hear the serpent speak, asked how he attained to human speech and such understanding not till now; the serpent answers, that by tasting of a certain tree in the garden he attained both to speech and reason, till then void of both: Eve requires him to bring her to that tree, and finds it to be the tree of knowledge forbidden. The serpent now

> grown bolder, with many wiles and arguments
> induces her at length to eat; she pleased with
> the taste deliberates awhile whether to impart
> thereof to Adam or not, at last brings him of
> the fruit, relates what persuaded her to eat
> thereof: Adam at first amazed, but perceiving
> her lost, resolves through vehemence of love
> to perish with her.

So, in Milton's account, Adam chooses sin out of his ardor for Eve, rather than because of deception. His mistake, of course, is in choosing her above God, for in that moment, he loses both. Continuing in the text, we read, "And extenuating the trespass, he eats also of the fruit. The effects thereof in them both, they seek to cover their nakedness, then fall to variance and accusation of one another." Immediately, they start arguing, the evidence that alienation has replaced relationship.

Before Satan seduces them with this momentous temptation, he laments the "pleasures about me, so much more I feel torment within me, as from the hateful siege of contraries; all good to me becomes bane." He is actually tempted not to continue this temptation, so overwhelmed is he by the exquisiteness of the created order, but he proceeds, of course. Milton goes on to describe, ignominiously, how this once angel, this once cherub, now has to descend and invade the body of a serpent—Satan is not exactly thrilled about this: "O foul descent! that I who erst contended with gods to sit the highest, am now constrained into a beast, and mixt with beastial slime, this essence to incarnate and imbrute, that to the height of deity aspired; but what will not ambition and revenge descend to?"

Note his point here. Ambition and revenge can lead us to commit acts we may have thought ourselves incapable of committing. He continues, "Who aspires must down as low as high he soared, obnoxious first or last to basest things." This is a powerful insight into the psychology of ambition and revenge. It also provides a brilliant and ironic contrast to the condescension of Christ in his incarnation. Satan, who has already become bestial because of his earlier rebellion against God's created order, resents his condescension merely from demon to serpent, while Christ condescended to become a man—the Creator a creature! The great mystery of the universe is how Christ, being fully God and fully human, would restrain himself to take on the limitations of fallen humanity. Furthermore, while Satan takes on the form of a serpent out of hate, Christ takes on the form of a man out of love, and in an irony that rivals all others, the Holy Spirit enables Mary to give birth to her own Maker and Savior because God's love transcends everything else. Milton seems to allude to these contrasts via the psychology of Satan here in book 9.

Later on in the book, there is a passage in which Adam and Eve discuss their fall. Eve accuses Adam of failing to lead properly: "Being as I am, why didst not thou the head command me absolutely not to go, going into such danger as thou saidst." In other words, she initially wanted to go alone, but now she complains that he let her go alone. She continues blaming him:

> Too facile then thou didst not much gainsay,
> nay didst permit, approve, and fair dismiss.
> Hadst thou been firm and fixed in thy dissent,
> neither had I transgressed, nor thou with me.
> To whom then first incensed Adam replied, Is
> this the love, is this the recompense of mine
> to thee, ingrateful Eve, expressed immutable
> when thou wert lost, not I, who might have
> lived and joyed immortal bliss, yet willingly
> chose rather death with thee: and am I now
> upbraided, as the cause of thy transgressing?
> Not enough severe, it seems, in thy restraint:
> what could I more? I warned thee, I admon-
> ished thee, foretold the danger, and the lurking
> enemy that lay in wait; beyond this had been
> force, and force upon free will hath here no
> place.

Notice, neither took responsibility for personal sin but condemned the other. The text goes on to say, "Thus they in mutual accusation spent the fruitless hours, but neither self-condemning, and of their vain contest appeared no end."

Book 10

In book 10 Milton wrote,

> He sends his son to judge the transgressors,
> who descends and gives sentence accordingly;
> then in pity clothes them both and re-ascends.
> Sin and Death sitting till then at the gates of

hell, by wondrous sympathy feeling the success of Satan in this new world, and the sin by
man there committed, resolve to sit no longer
confined in hell, but to follow Satan, their
sire, up to the place of man: to make the way
easier from hell to this world to and fro, they
pave a broad highway or bridge over Chaos,
according to the track that Satan first made;
then preparing for earth, they meet him proud
of his success returning to hell; their mutual
gratulation. Satan arrives at Pandemonium, in
full assembly relates with boasting his success
against man; instead of applause is entertained
with a general hiss by all his audience.

The reason for the hissing is that they have all become
serpents. Then a tree of life emerges before them. When they
greedily reach for the fruit, they find they only "chew dust
and bitter ashes." Apparently, they transform into serpents
on a regular basis.

At the very end of book 10, Adam and Eve repent: "What
better can we do, than to the place repairing where He judged
us, prostrate fall before Him reverent, and there confess
humbly our faults, and pardon beg, with tears watering the
ground." So, they come to the point of repentance and contrition. We see "the Son of God presents to his father the prayers
of our first parents now repenting, and intercedes for them:
God accepts them, but declares that they must no longer abide
in Paradise; sends Michael with a band of cherubim to dispos-
sess them; but first to reveal to Adam future things."

Book 11

This book begins, "Thus they in lowliest plight repentant stood praying, for from the mercy-seat above prevenient grace [a grace that is previous to the response] descending had removed the stony from their hearts, and made new flesh regenerate grow instead, that sighs now breathed unutterable, which the spirit of prayer inspired, and winged for heaven with speedier flight than loudest oratory."

At the end of this material, we find the Son of God interceding on behalf of Adam and Eve: "Of paradise could have produced, ere fallen from innocence. Now therefore bend thine ear to supplication, hear his sighs though mute; unskilful with what words to pray, let me interpret for him, me his advocate and propitiation, all his works on me good or not good engraft, my merit those shall perfect, and for these my death shall pay. Accept me, and in me from these receive the smell of peace toward mankind, let him live before thee reconciled." Milton acknowledged the priestly role of Christ in the biblical symbolism he incorporated here. Christ covers the couple with skins, symbolizing the sacrificial system that will exist in the interim between the fall and the incarnation of Christ. He intercedes on their behalf, representing Christ's role as High Priest, as well as the later function of the Holy Spirit as Comforter and Intercessor. Milton made every attempt to remain true to the Bible even in his elaboration on it.

Book 12

The material concludes with an extraordinary portrait, moving from Adam to the flood, then to Abraham, then to the coming of Christ, his work, his resurrection, and then to the anticipation of Christ's second coming. At the end of book 12, Adam makes this comment: "O goodness infinite, goodness immense! That all this good of evil shall produce, and evil turn to good; more wonderful than that which by creation first brought forth light out of darkness!" In other words, he asserts that in the mystery of the sovereignty of God, a good—even greater than what was there before—has been wrought out of this ill.

The last lines of the poem emphasize the consequences of sin and Adam and Eve's expulsion from Paradise. While they are not without a dimension of hope, having heard the future that God has prepared for them, Milton highlighted the pain of their loss of Paradise. He concluded his epic by depicting the young couple's hesitant departure from the garden: "They looking back, all the eastern side beheld of paradise, so late their happy seat, waved over by that flaming brand, the gate with dreadful faces thronged and fiery arms: some natural tears they dropped, but wiped them soon; the world was all before them, where to choose their place of rest, and providence their guide: they hand in hand with wandering steps and slow, through Eden took their solitary way." Even in these final lines, Milton maintained his theological purpose. He reminded the reader that we, like Adam and Eve, "choose [our] place of rest" and are guided by providence.

The consequences of the rebel will are obvious, yet God has not abandoned his creation. Like Adam and Eve, the world is all before us, and we must choose in whom or what to rest.

Final Thoughts

One of my overarching thoughts about *Paradise Lost* is the wonderful way in which it illustrates and illuminates the human condition. I believe this book shows, through the use of emotions and vivid imagery, how the fall into sin happens in our own lives and how we ought to live in light of this. I agree with Aristotle: "Intellect of itself 'moves nothing': the transition from thinking to doing . . . needs to be assisted by appropriate states of feeling" (*A Preface to Paradise Lost*, 53).

In the ancient world, rhetoric consisted of three elements; it combined passion and reason to compel action. Similarly, poetry calls on emotion to support an imaginative vision that promotes wisdom. Poetry can build spiritual health when it is written in a soul-enriching, truth-enhancing way. This is what Milton sought to do. His imaginative vision touches our emotions and elevates our minds into spheres of comprehension and experience we might not otherwise attain; it also gives us a sense of connection with the created order and with the One for whom we were created.

I would suggest, as well, that there is an analogy between the Christian and the creative life. It is this: a Christian has to work hard at living a Christian life, in terms of the disciplines of the faith. Yet the one essential act of the Christian life is the surrender of the will. In a very interesting way poets must work hard at their craft, and yet their greatest achievements are not theirs, but they are inspired by surrendering the will, as it were. I hope that we would take away from this epic poem the desire to surrender our own rebellious wills and selfish ideas about life and, instead, embrace the mysterious counsels of God, because "no eye has seen, no ear has heard, no mind has conceived what God has prepared for those who love him" (1 Corinthians 2:9 NIV).

Father, we thank you for this work of excellence and of insight, which can provide us an imaginative way of understanding the nature of the spiritual life. I pray that all of us would come to understand better the issues of our own temptations, our own rationalizations, and our own ambitions to get life on our own terms. I pray that we would joyfully submit to the path of contrition, repentance, and obedience and affirm that your will is, indeed, our perfect freedom. We pray in Christ's name. Amen.

NOTES

Confessions

Introduction

The *Confessions* of Augustine is an extraordinary achievement of devotional, philosophical, and theological literature that both inspires the mind and inflames the heart. Throughout these confessions, Augustine wrote as though speaking directly to God, couching his thoughts in the form of prayers. It is evident that he was acutely aware of God's presence and viewed God as relevant to every component of his life.

Aurelius Augustinus was a man who stood at a major crossroads of history. By the time he was born (AD 354), the Roman Empire was already in the process of internal decay and disintegration. The Goths, the Visigoths, and the Vandals were moving down from northern Europe and getting perilously close to Rome itself. By the time of Augustine's death (AD 430), the Vandals had actually crossed the Mediterranean Sea— not content with conquests on the European continent—and were in North Africa. In fact, it is reported that Augustine died as the very walls of his city were being breached. And so, as the Roman Empire crumbled, Augustine reflected on history, theology, and his relationship with God.

Near the end of his life, Augustine returned to his home in northern Africa and became the bishop of Hippo (Hippo Regius is present-day Annaba, Algeria). One challenge that he addressed concerned the idea that Christianity had corrupted the Roman Empire by causing Rome to abandon its gods. Some Romans saw the weakening of the empire and the numerous invasions as divine punishment for having forgotten their deities. In response to this argument, Augustine wrote *The City of God*, in which he put forward the first Christian philosophy of history. He contrasted the metaphoric city of God with the cities or governments of humanity, arguing that ultimately the city of God alone would prevail. He asserted that nations rise and fall, but God is the one who triumphs.

The City of God produced an enormous impact on church history. Augustine's synthesis—both philosophical and theological—guided the church during many dark years of apparent chaos. The church continued to be the harbinger and the preserver of culture—the Greek and Latin classics and theology. Augustine's writings blended the Greco-Roman heritage with the Judeo-Christian scriptural traditions and greatly influenced the development of Western thought.

In this way, he is seen as bridging the gap between ancient Rome and the Christian Middle Ages. *Confessions* remains a treasured work and can be read in a variety of translations.

The word *confession* typically connotes the confession of sins, and while that is surely one of the components of the book, another component involves the confession of the Christian faith in a rather unique form. By reflecting on his life, Augustine composed a spiritual and intellectual auto-biography—a profession of faith and a declaration of God's glory. He confessed his own sins, he confessed the truth of Christianity, and he also confessed the glory, goodness, beauty, and greatness of the living God. One man's life, then, became a means of demonstrating a vibrant faith. His experience can be viewed as a microcosm—a life in miniature—of what it is like for those who have been alienated from God to then be wooed back to God. This book presents God as the lover of our souls who is always calling us to return to him. In Augustine's case, God pursued him for many years. Augustine described his own experience: "I have learnt to love you late, Beauty at once so ancient and so new! I have learnt to love you late!"

Another dimension of this material involves its presentation of a man engaged in a spiritual journey—on a quest for truth. He reminds me of a very recent philosopher, Mortimer Adler, who considered all possible philosophical options in his quest for truth. As each philosophical view proved inadequate, he gradually concluded that there had to be some kind of a truth, some kind of an answer, some kind of an absolute. His journey led, by slow degrees, away from an agnostic position to a theistic one. He finally opted for Christianity because it provided the meaning he sought. Similarly, Augustine's *Confessions* relates a comparable intellectual and spiritual quest.

Life Sketch

Augustine was born in the small, backwater province of Thagaste, in the Roman Empire, and his life is the story of a local boy who made good. His father soon realized that his boy was unusually gifted and, having great ambitions for him, sacrificed to send him to school in nearby Madaurus (a Numidian city about nineteen miles from Thagaste), so he could learn what were then called the *liberal arts*. In Latin, this term literally means "the skills suitable for a free man (*libera*)," as opposed to the skills of a slave or a person who worked in a trade. The liberal arts trained students to become thinking citizens and made them capable of advancing in society.

As a youth, Augustine first learned the basic skills of grammar, rhetoric, and dialectic (logic). Grammar essentially entailed learning how to read, understand, interpret, and apply classical texts. Rhetoric prepared a student to speak publicly in a persuasive and convincing manner. It included study of voice, intonation, and gestures. The third area, logic, trained the student in the techniques of analysis and argumentation. These three subjects were termed the *trivium*, from which our modern word *trivial* is derived. In contrast to the denotation of that word today, however, in the classical world, *trivium* connoted those areas of study that were common and essential. The confluence of these three areas of study was considered a prerequisite for any educated man of that era, and the trivium provided the foundation for the next level of study. During this phase a student advanced to abstract analysis of arithmetic and geometry as applied to astronomy and music. These four subjects were termed the *quadrivium* and combined with the trivium to compose the seven liberal arts.

Augustine's particular focus was in rhetoric. He aspired to become a professor of rhetoric and a paid communicator who could advance in his career. Although a brilliant student, young Augustine became involved in sexual promiscuity and was also influenced by astrology and other false teachings. All this was a great source of grief to his mother, Monica, a devout Christian who passionately prayed for her son's conversion. Years before, while Augustine was still quite young, he had become seriously ill. Fearing he might die, Monica had deliberated over having him baptized. He recovered, however, and she chose to delay baptism. At this time, church teaching held that baptism would erase all past sins but not provide for future sins; therefore, people often delayed baptism until late in life—even until the deathbed. Fortunately, God spared Augustine, and Monica continued to pray for his salvation while, by his own account, Augustine wasted the next fifteen years of his life in a misspent youth.

As a young man, Augustine rejected his mother's faith in favor of false teachings. Manichaeism, in particular, intrigued Augustine; it was a third-century heresy similar to Gnosticism. Its founder, Mani, was of Jewish origin, and he proposed a synthesis of all the religious systems of the time. According to Manichaean doctrine, good and evil exist as eternal and equal powers, and matter is believed to be corrupted or evil. It taught that through meditation followers could free themselves from the evil matter of their bodies and achieve a unity between their immaterial souls and the divine. This heresy failed to regard God as omnipotent, so therefore he was viewed as incapable of effectively dealing with the problem of evil.

This is essentially the same argument that was popularized in Rabbi Kushner's best-selling book *When Bad Things Happen to Good People* (Avon, 1981). His thesis essentially suggested that if God was all-powerful, he would stop evil; since evil exists, God must not be all-powerful. This same dilemma greatly perplexed Augustine and inclined him toward Manichaeism. Sadly, the Manichaeans, Augustine, and Kushner (though for different reasons) all fell prey to faulty reasoning, and ironically, Augustine's liberal arts education failed to aid him in comprehending this faulty syllogism. As C. S. Lewis noted in *Mere Christianity*, the Manichaean dualistic view of the universe depends on good and evil being equal in strength and independent from each other. Lewis explained that supposedly they "both existed from all eternity. Neither of them made the other, neither of them has any more right than the other to call itself God. Each presumably thinks it is good and thinks the other bad. One of them likes hatred and cruelty, the other likes love and mercy" (*Mere Christianity* [New York: HarperCollins, 2001], 42). Lewis went on to point out how illogical this argument ultimately becomes, for both depend on some kind of standard by which we judge what is good and what is bad. He continued,

> Now if we mean merely that we happen to prefer the first, then we must give up talking about good and evil at all. For good means what you ought to prefer quite regardless of what you happen to like at any given moment. If "being good" meant simply joining the side you happened to fancy, for no real reason, then good would not deserve to be called good. So we must mean that one of the two powers is actually wrong and the other actually right.
>
> But the moment you say that, you are putting into the universe a third thing in addition to the two Powers: some law or standard or rule of good which one of the powers conforms to and the other fails to conform to. But since the two powers are judged by this standard, then this standard, or the Being who made this standard, is farther back and higher up than either of them, and He will be the real God. In fact, what we meant by calling them good and bad turns out to be that one of them is in a right relationship to the real ultimate God and the other in a wrong relation to Him. (43)

Lewis further argued that for any dualistic worldview to be true, the bad power must actually prefer badness for its own sake, but we cannot find any such cases in the real world. He asserted that people are motivated to evil either by sadism—a perverted enjoyment of cruelty—or by some perceived benefit to themselves, such as power. Yet even here dualism fails, for sadism *is*, in a sick way, a type of enjoyment or power. So, logically, sadistic persons are attempting to gain "a good" through the pursuit of evil. From this we can infer, as did Lewis (and Augustine later in his life), that evil is a distorted pursuit of good. To quote Lewis, "Goodness is, so to speak, itself: badness is only spoiled goodness. . . . In order to be bad [one] must have good things to want and then to pursue in the wrong way: he must have impulses which were originally good in order to be able to pervert them. But if he is bad he cannot supply himself either with good things to desire or with good impulses to pervert. He must be getting both from the Good Power. And if so, then he is not independent" (44). It took Augustine many years to finally realize these essential flaws of the dualistic Manichaean heresy, and during that time he struggled to resist God and the guilt of his own convictions.

At age seventeen Augustine moved to Carthage to continue his study of rhetoric. There he struggled with sexual temptation and sensualism. In his own words, "I went to Carthage, where I found myself in the midst of a hissing cauldron of lust. I had not yet fallen in love, but I was in love with the idea of it." Augustine indulged his lusts but remained unhappy. During this time he took a concubine and had a son, Adeodatus. It appears he loved his concubine deeply, and they remained together for the next fifteen years. At age nineteen, Augustine returned to Thagaste to teach rhetoric, but after only two years he moved back to Carthage to conduct a school of rhetoric there. Augustine continued to seek gratification and success rather than God.

After nine years in Carthage and against the wishes of his mother, Augustine decided to go to Rome. Almost immediately he became gravely ill, and he later reflected on God's grace that preserved him when he "was a fool who laughed at the cure which you prescribed when you saved me, in my state of sin, from twofold death, the death of the body and the death of the soul." After his recovery Augustine taught literature and public speaking, drawing the attention of a prefect of Rome who had been asked to find a rhetoric and elocution teacher for the imperial court at Milan. Augustine received this prestigious appointment and moved to Milan at age thirty. God's pursuit of Augustine was particularly evident in this stage of his life: the move marked his final break with the Manichaeans; his godly mother moved to Milan to be near him; and while there he became influenced by the writings of the apostle Paul through the teaching of Ambrose, the bishop of Milan.

Initially, Augustine merely desired to emulate Ambrose's masterful style of rhetoric, but he soon became more impressed by Ambrose's ability to interpret the Scriptures in a spiritual rather than merely allegorical sense. Under this man's influence, Augustine realized that although he loved Cicero and Virgil and would weep over the departure of Aeneas from Dido, he had never wept over his own sins. He loved Latin literature, but when he had read the Scriptures, he had not been impressed and had set them aside. However, when he heard the Scriptures communicated by Ambrose, he was drawn to them. As he began to study the Bible, he realized that Scripture contained many layers and levels of meaning, and he was intrigued by the profound truths they revealed.

In addition to Ambrose, the writings of the apostle Paul proved another profound influence when Augustine decided to attend catechesis—an elementary form of religious instruction—even though he was not yet a true believer in Jesus Christ. As he learned more about the Christian faith, Paul's epistles greatly influenced him.

Although Augustine served in a prestigious position within the Roman Empire, an accepted method of advancement in society was to marry an independently wealthy woman from a good family. If a young man came from a humble background, as Augustine did, then an arranged marriage could quickly advance his career and status. Augustine struggled with ambition, so he allowed his mother to arrange a social marriage; however, this marriage never took place. By necessity it was delayed for two years until the young woman was of marriageable age, and during that time Augustine's life direction changed dramatically. In preparation for the marriage, a heartbroken Augustine sent his concubine back to Africa while their son remained in Milan with him. Out of devotion to Augustine, the concubine vowed to live celibate for the remainder of her life; but Augustine, by his own admission, failed to subdue his lust for even the two-year period before his marriage. Almost immediately after his concubine returned to Africa, he took another. Although he lamented his weakness, he continued to indulge it.

Augustine rightly believed that the Greek and Roman philosophers had a rather naive view of the human ability to use reason to attain virtue, and he concluded that reason-based self-control was an arrogant and unrealistically optimistic route. Ironically, in part because of the writings of pagan philosophers and in part because of the respective influences of Ambrose and Scripture, he realized his sexual promiscuity was the very excuse he was using to keep himself from knowing God and from making that decision of the will to abandon himself—even if it meant living a celibate life and never advancing in his career.

Augustine wrote about how his lust was an impediment that kept him from God: "As a youth I had been woefully at fault, particularly in early adolescence. I had prayed to you for chastity and said 'Give me chastity and continence, but not yet.' For I was afraid that you would answer my prayer at once and cure me too soon the disease of lust, which I wanted satisfied, not quelled." I am struck by that honesty because it really provided an antidote to his pride. Reflecting in his *Confessions*, Augustine was able to assess and admit his motives as he struggled with sexual impurity. This demonstrates an amazing level of self-awareness.

Augustine's conversion to the Christian faith took place after he heard a story about a Platonist philosopher who gave up everything to convert to Christianity. At this man's baptismal ceremony, he made a profession of faith that ended his respected philosophy career. This account inspired Augustine, and through this process I can almost see the "hound of heaven" closing in on him. Finally, the spiritual transformation occurred.

After his conversion Augustine and his son were baptized by Ambrose during Easter of 387. He then decided to abandon his career in rhetoric, quit his teaching position in Milan, forgo any ideas of marriage, and devote himself entirely to serving God through the practices of the priesthood, which included celibacy. He decided to return to his home in Africa, but heartache soon followed, for his mother died along the way, and his son died soon after their arrival in Africa.

Upon returning to North Africa, Augustine gave his money to the poor and kept only the family house, which he converted into a monastic foundation. He became a priest in 391 and received the appointment as bishop of Hippo in 396. He remained in this position until his death in 430. He spent his last years writing and speaking to convince others of the truth of the Christian faith.

Style

Confessions may be regarded as something of an autobiography, but it also retraces an intellectual and spiritual journey. Augustine offered his past experiences and his present life as illustrations of God's pursuit and grace. He came clean, so to speak, before God and people so that he could become a person of integrity. His honesty resonates with us; we can relate to his conflicts, for we all struggle with essentially the same issues.

Augustine addressed God in praise and in admission of weakness. The style constantly moves in and out of what might be called different "registers"—or stylistically unique entries. Even within a sentence, he may move from impassioned prayer to quiet narrative. Then he might transition into a quotation or a combination of Bible texts here and there. Occasionally, he may engage in a philosophical analysis of a problem or go to a prayer or invoke some classical literature. The book is rich and very diverse. We can use the term *polyphonic discourse* to describe Augustine's writing, for it is like music coming from many sources. It is layered, and it dances and responds almost like a counterpoint. His work first maps his journey away from his home and from his God and then, ultimately, his return to truth.

He abruptly ended the autobiographical portion of *Confessions* with his conversion and the death of his mother, although he wrote it fifteen years after those events. A typical autobiography would bring the reader up to the time of the writing, but I believe that he constructed his book in this way because he wanted the reader to grasp that his spiritual awakening was the pivotal point of his life. Surprisingly, instead of continuing on with his own story, he then diverged into a discourse on memory, time, and creation; and in the last books he provided an exposition on the first few verses of Genesis.

Many people have wondered why he did that. I suggest that books 1 through 9 were intended to relate his past and the journey up to the point of his conversion. There Augustine chronicled the path by which he came to understand his own inadequacy. Then book 10 and following served to examine his postsalvation growth process. In book 10 he emphasized how he came to know God. In the remaining books he focused on the pursuit of knowledge of God. My own argument is that we cannot know ourselves unless we know God. I think that is why Augustine then used the remaining books to focus on the basics of the faith and to compose a rich theology, beginning with the first chapter of Genesis. He provided the reader with a catechesis of theology in those last chapters, and they serve an important purpose in his exposition. He asked some tough questions and moved on into a philosophical discourse at that point. Then his pursuit of knowledge of God and creation brought him to the study of Genesis. He noted, "In the beginning God created the heaven and the earth," but what was the beginning? So in books 11 through 13, he explored God's relationship to time and space.

Surely, Augustine possessed an unusual degree of self-awareness. I am particularly struck by the way he analyzed his motivations—the way he was able to think about and explore why he did what he did. He realized that although he engaged in all kinds of selfish pursuits, God purposefully used them to reveal that his hope was misplaced.

Influence

This book, in my opinion, influenced a wide variety of other writers, from Boethius to Dante and from Pascal to Cardinal Newman. I even think it influenced Marcel Proust in his *Remembrance of Things Past*. All these writers share something in common: they were amazed at the process of recollection and how processing past occurrences can be affected by present experience. Yet Proust, for example, did not rely on any strength but his own, and he ultimately sought his answers only in literature and the inner journey, rather than in the quest for the living God. In contrast, I think that Augustine wanted his readers to look at themselves in the light of their relationship to the living God.

I want to review some highlights from the thirteen books that compose *Confessions*. I will focus on select passages that are among my favorites and provide a brief summary of this material.

Book 1

In book 1 Augustine praised God's greatness and wisdom. He also wrote about his mother, Monica, and the fifteen years of his life that he wasted apart from God. He related the influence of Virgil's writings on his life and thought and examined his awareness of sin. Concerning his sins, he asked, "Were they just peccadilloes [little sins]? No, they were worse than that." In reflection, he saw them as being the very beginning of a process of selfish aggrandizement—of trying to impress his friends and live life independently from God.

Let me share just a few selections from book 1. He began with a remarkable prayer.

> "Can any praise be worthy of the Lord's majesty?" (Psalm 145:3). "How magnificent his strength! How inscrutable his wisdom!" (Psalm 147:5). Man is one of your creatures, Lord, and his instinct is to praise you. He bears about him the mark of death, the sign of his own sin, to remind him that you "thwart the proud" (1 Peter

5:5). But still, since he is a part of your creation, he wishes to praise you. The thought of you stirs him so deeply that he cannot be content unless he praises you, because you made us for yourself and our hearts find no peace until they rest in you.

That last sentence is one of the best-known lines from this book: "You made us for yourself and our hearts find no peace until they rest in you." That is, by the way, the essence of this whole book. The rest of the book describes his utter restlessness and apparent futility in his desire to find the truth.

In another part of book 1, he considered a long litany of paradoxical statements about God.

You are the most hidden from us and yet the most present amongst us, the most beautiful and yet the most strong, ever enduring and yet we cannot comprehend you. You are unchangeable and yet you change all things. You are never new, never old, and yet all things have new life from you. You are the unseen power that brings decline upon the proud. You are ever active, yet always at rest. You gather all things to yourself, though you suffer no need. You support, you fill, and you protect all things. You create them, nourish them, and bring them to perfection. You seek to make them your own, though you lack for nothing. You love your creatures, but with a gentle love. You treasure them, but without apprehension. You grieve for wrong, but suffer no pain. You

can be angry and yet serene. Your works are
varied, but your purpose is one and the same. ,
You welcome all who come to you, though
you never lost them.

One of the things that I love about Augustine is that he
recognized that despite humanity's best efforts, God remains
a deep and profound mystery. Yet he always wanted to press
ever further and higher into that mystery. Furthermore,
he grasped that God's love for his creation is at the heart
of that mystery. "It is a created order," he wrote, and it is
"profoundly mysterious." He was awed by a God who loved
out of complete sufficiency.

He went on to say, "For you are infinite and never change.
In you 'today' never comes to an end: and yet our 'today'
does come to and end in you, because time, and everything
else, exists in you. If it did not, it would have no means of
passing. And since your years never come to an end, for you
they are simply 'today'. The countless days of our lives and
of our forefathers' lives have passed by within your 'today.'"
He then meditated on this mystery of time. So this first book
is essentially a profound analysis of the nature of Augustine's
early experiences.

Book 2

In the second book, he recalled his past carnal corrup-
tions, and these recollections were very painful to him. He
told about his youth and early experiences and about his education in Carthage. Instead of delving into descriptions of his

carnal problems and his dissolutions, he focused instead on a particular time when he and some friends decided to steal some pears. I think the reason he did this was so he could fully exploit all the angles, all the machinations of the act. He acknowledged that he was not motivated by desire for the pears because, as he admitted, they were actually quite ordinary. He was motivated by the sin itself. As he later examined his heart, he asked, "What was it, then, that pleased me in that act of theft? Which of my Lord's powers did I imitate in a perverse and wicked way? . . . Could I enjoy doing wrong for no other reason than that it was wrong?" He came to the sobering conclusion that his enjoyment of theft represented a perverse enjoyment of the illusion of power. At the heart of all sin is a desire to play God.

He analyzed the nature of sin by taking what would appear to be a mundane experience and using it to reveal the depth of his depravity. He went on to discuss how an individual might seem to escape the consequences of the theft of a few pears but not the consequences of sexual immorality. He used the incident as a symbol of a far more profound reality: each of us constantly struggles with an attraction to various types of sin in his or her own life journey.

He continued to explain, "So the soul defiles itself with unchaste love when it turns away from you and looks elsewhere for things which it cannot find pure and unsullied except by returning to you. All who desert you and set themselves up against you merely copy you in a perverse way; but by this very act of imitation they only show that you are the Creator of all nature and, consequently, that there is no place whatever where man may hide away from you." Even when we try to avoid God, we are looking for him in a distorted search. Even our quest for pleasure is an exploitation of the created order, which points beyond itself to the living God. Augustine then reflected on the impact of this distorted search on his own life and understanding in the remaining sections of this book.

Book 3

In book 3 we learn that Augustine spent his seventeenth through his nineteenth years at Carthage, which was the capital of North Africa. In the description of his time there, he stated, "I found myself in the midst of a hissing cauldron of lust." Not only was this a time of physical temptation for young Augustine, but this is also when he fell into the error of Manichaeism. What he did not understand at that age was that evil is not a substance that has being, but it is a nonbeing or lacks being, and thus has no devil creator to rival God.

At first he had thought that evil is a substance. His misconception was that God created everything, including evil, and if God created evil, then either God cannot be good or he cannot be sovereign. Therefore, the Manichaean doctrine of an evil force and a good force appealed to him. He failed to realize that evil is not a substance or entity but merely a perversion of a good—a privation, rather than a thing itself. This is a key concept in the Augustinian analysis of good and evil. Another Manichaean error that Augustine struggled with was the belief that God exists in time and space. Misunderstanding both God's sovereignty over his creation, as well as his spirit form, he explained, "I did not know that God is a spirit, a being without bulk and without limbs defined in length and breadth."

This section of *Confessions* also chronicles Augustine's frustration with the Bible. Speaking about his experiences as he read the Scriptures, Augustine admitted, "To me they seemed quite unworthy of comparison with the stately prose of Cicero, because I had too much conceit to accept their simplicity and not enough insight to penetrate their depths. It is surely true that as the child grows these books grow with him. But I was too proud to call myself a child. I was inflated with self-esteem, which made me think myself a great man." Once again he explored how, in his folly, he had deceived himself.

At the end of book 3, he described a vision experienced by his mother. Distraught with her son's adherence to the Manichaean heresy, she had a vision that her son would ultimately come to faith. Yet even a vision did not ease her heart, for Monica appealed to a bishop of the church to go and speak with Augustine. Augustine later recalled, "My mother still would not be pacified, but persisted all the more with her tears and her entreaties that he [the bishop] should see me and discuss the matter. At last he grew impatient and said 'Leave me and go in peace. It cannot be that the son of these tears should be lost.'" In reflection, Augustine stated that he believed the bishop's refusal reflected God's intervention, for he was "unripe" for instruction. Even so, the fact is that he was gradually drawn to the faith by the prayers of this godly woman.

I think it is good for all of us to consider what influences various people have had on our lives. If we have accepted Jesus

Christ as our Lord and Savior, we can be assured that there were people praying for us throughout that conversion process. I heard an anecdote about a person coming to Christ while flying on an airplane. A fellow traveler—a complete stranger—took the initiative to present an entirely different worldview, and the Holy Spirit then drew the person to Christ. I am amazed when I hear of such encounters, and yet I am confident that the life-changing event was not the individual's first exposure to the gospel. Someone had already been watering that soil and preparing the way, just as Monica's prayers prepared the way for Augustine to come to faith.

Book 4

In book 4 we learn that at age eighteen, Augustine settled down to teach rhetoric in his hometown of Thagaste in what is now eastern Algeria. This is where he took on his mistress, whom he kept for fifteen years but never named—deliberately, it would appear, in an effort to preserve her honor. Upon the sudden death of a very dear friend, Augustine left Thagaste and its sad memories and returned to Carthage. There he began to read the writings of Aristotle, as well as speeches of the Roman orator Hierius. He was impressed by their visions of beauty, and when he was about twenty, Augustine actually wrote a few books on this topic as he struggled to comprehend the source of beauty. He questioned, "What is it that attracts us and wins us over to the things we love?" Like so many others, the young Augustine succumbed to admiration of God's created world and its good gifts and failed to see God himself as the true source of beauty.

One of my favorite quotes is from book 4. In it the mature Augustine stated, "'O God of hosts, restore us to our own; smile upon us, and we shall find deliverance' (Psalm 79:8). For wherever the soul of man may turn, unless it turns to you, it clasps sorrow to itself. Even though it clings to things of beauty, if their beauty is outside God and outside the soul, it only clings to sorrow." It is a wonderful image, is it not, of clasping sorrow to ourselves? It also reveals Augustine's proper understanding of beauty's source and function.

In another passage he wrote, "If the things of this world delight you, praise God for them but turn your love away from them and give it to their Maker." This is a rather interesting notion. We live in a wondrous world, and though it is fallen, it is full of beauty, splendor, order, and design. If we truly enjoy something, let it point us to our Creator. Augustine continued by clarifying why we should love God, not merely his creation: "So that in the things that please you you may not displease him. If your delight is in souls, love them in God."

Here is another interesting idea: we must love people and things *in God*. Augustine discussed the secret to learning to love God rather than things. He argued, "The good things which you love are all from God, but they are good and sweet only as long as they are used to do his will. They will rightly turn bitter if God is spurned and the things that come from him are wrongly loved." He implied that we can love God when we love a person, in our service or through our work.

We can love God in the most ordinary and mundane kinds of activities. By doing this, we transmute the ordinary and turn it into the extraordinary—we turn the secular into the spiritual. This process of transmutation is achieved by loving and enjoying God himself rather than just his good gifts. Augustine provided ample explanation for why we should love God: "our Life himself came down into this world and took away our death. He slew it with his own abounding life, and with thunder in his voice he called us from this world to return to him in heaven."

Book 5

In the next book Augustine discussed the process by which he was finally able to escape from his nine-year adherence to the erroneous doctrine of Manichaeism. When he was twenty-nine, a Manichaean bishop named Faustus, a man who was touted for his knowledge, wisdom, and insight, came to Carthage. Augustine had anticipated that Faustus would answer his questions concerning some of the inconsistencies within Manichaeism; however, Faustus proved to be an incredible disappointment because of his weak scholarship and character. Augustine realized that he knew far more about the liberal arts and science than this man did. Following this encounter, he came under the influence of Ambrose and benefited from his perspective on the writings of the apostle Paul. This life-altering relationship occurred after Augustine left both Manichaeism and Carthage and moved to Rome. He went to Rome to teach literature and rhetoric but was soon recommended for a position in Milan. While in Milan he became acquainted with Ambrose, the city's bishop, and through him, the writings of Paul. Although Augustine found the answers offered by the church to be much better than those of the Manichaeans, he remained a skeptic. He explained, "For I thought the Catholic side unbeaten but still not victorious."

Book 6

In book 6 Augustine wrote that his mother had joined him in Milan. He was still struggling spiritually and continued to crave honors and success, as we all do in this world. We are constantly torn between the claims of the temporal and the eternal. This constant pull of the will is something Augustine vividly described. Like him, many of his friends were dabbling in religion and proved to be powerful influences as well. It was during this time that he reluctantly sent his mistress back to Africa because he had agreed to a socially beneficial marriage, yet his sexual struggles continued. Almost immediately, he took another mistress. Although he felt guilty, he indulged his lust, admitting he "was more a slave of lust than a true lover of marriage." Augustine recorded his analysis of this period of his life. He stated, "And I never wondered what was the source of my pleasure in discussing these topics, shameful as they were . . . nor did I ask myself why, however great my indulgence in sensual pleasure, I could not find happiness, even in the sense in which I then conceived of it." Clearly, Augustine struggled to find purpose and satisfaction in life. He concluded book 6 by acknowledging God's sufficiency: "You are there to free us from the misery of error which leads us astray, to set us on your own path and to comfort us by saying, 'Run on, for I shall hold you up. I shall lead you and carry you on to the end.'"

All of us have a fatal flaw, maybe even more than one. When I think about my own life, I realize that when I came to Christ, some vices fell away immediately. Then there were other habits and desires that changed gradually, and I gained victory over them. But there is also a third kind of a struggle. This type is like gristle. It's something I keep chewing on, but I can never quite get rid of it. In other words, we must endure some struggles for as long as we live in this world. Paul spoke to such issues when he warned, "Therefore let him who thinks he stands take heed that he does not fall" (1 Corinthians 10:12).

It is unwise to put any confidence in the flesh. In this life the flesh is never going to be perfected or removed. The fact is we shouldn't even try to clean it up. Instead we should invite Jesus to reign supreme over it. We must walk by his power and with the Spirit rather than trying to shape up and improve our flesh. It just doesn't work that way. I think Augustine discovered this very painfully.

Books 7 and 8

In the seventh book Augustine, at the age of thirty, recounted that he began to read a great deal of Plato's philosophy, which ironically led him to conclude that God is

omniscient and exists as pure spirit. He later realized that
God used even pagan Platonic philosophies to bring him to
a greater understanding of the concepts that would prepare
him for true faith. This was a significant step in preparing his
heart for salvation. The mystery of the origin of evil had long
been a stumbling block for Augustine. He wrongly attributed
evil to essentially three possibilities: (1) There is something
evil in the matter from which God made the universe. (2)
Evil exists because God lacks the omnipotence to destroy it.
(3) God is not good because he has not annihilated evil. Yet
once Augustine grasped that God exists in spirit form and is
not contained in or by his creation, he began to comprehend
the infinity and sovereignty of God. He wrote, "When I asked
myself what wickedness was, I saw that it was not a substance
but perversion of the will when it turns aside from you, O
God, who are the supreme substance."

In book eight Augustine noted that when he was thirty-
one years of age, he heard about a professor by the name of
Victorinus, who had sacrificed his career to become a Christian.
He also learned of several other Roman officials who made
similar kinds of sacrifices, and their examples inspired him.
While he was still struggling with his own issues and difficulties, he was converted to Christ in a very powerful way. He
spoke of it this way: "My thoughts, as I meditated upon you,
were like the efforts of a man who tries to wake but cannot
and sinks back into the depths of slumber. No one wants to
sleep for ever, for everyone rightly agrees that it is better to
be awake. Yet a man often staves off the effort to rouse himself
when his body is leaden with inertia."

Have you ever had that experience? You feel like you're hinged to the rack, and you can't get out of it? There are actions you know you should take, and yet you find yourself pulled down by the gravity—by the inertia of the flesh. Likewise Augustine noted, "I was quite sure that it was better for me to give myself up to your love than to surrender to my own lust. But while I wanted to follow the first course and was convinced that it was right, I was a slave to the pleasures of the second." He observed, "For the rule of sin is the force of habit, by which the mind is swept along and held fast even against its will." He habituated this most of his life and discussed how this issue came down to an act of the will, and a volitional response of submission was required.

That volitional response came in an unusual way. Augustine described "a small garden attached to the house where we lodged. We were free to make use of it as well as the rest of the house because our host, the owner of the house, did not live there." Augustine and his friend Alypius would often go out into the garden and reflect. At one point while he was in the garden, he felt the pull of the Spirit, which later prompted him to ask, "Why does this strange phenomenon occur? What causes it? O Lord in your mercy give me light to see, for it may be that the answer to my question lies in the secret punishment of man and in the penitence which casts a deep shadow on the sons of Adam. Why does this strange phenomenon occur? What causes it? The mind gives an order to the body and is at once obeyed, but when it gives an order to itself, it is resisted."

Have you ever noticed that struggle? As Augustine observed, "The mind commands the hand to move and is so readily obeyed that the order can scarcely be distinguished from its execution. Yet the mind is mind and the hand is part of the body. But when the mind commands the mind to make an act of will, these two are one in the same and yet the order is not obeyed." I know exactly what he was talking about. One of the things I love about Augustine is that he never took anything for granted. He was constantly asking questions about things I often don't wonder about. He noted, "The mind orders itself to make an act of will, and it would not give this order unless it willed to do so; yet it does not carry out its own command. But it does not fully will to do this thing and therefore its orders are not fully given. It gives the order only in so far as it wills, and in so far as it does not will the order is not carried out."

Then he came to the crux of the matter. He realized that he stood on the brink of resolution. How long would he put off a decision? He later explained, "I could not reach out to it or grasp it, because I held back from the step by which I should die to death and become alive to life. My lower instincts, which had taken firm hold of me, were stronger than the higher, which were untried. And the closer I came to the moment which was to mark the great change in me, the more I shrank from it in horror. But it did not drive me back or turn me from my purpose: it merely left me hanging in suspense."

Although he had arrived at this point, he could not make the move. So God in his grace intervened in a truly special way. Augustine described what happened next.

> I kept crying, "How long shall I go on saying 'tomorrow, tomorrow'? Why not now? Why

not make an end of my ugly sins at this moment?" I was asking myself these questions,
weeping all the while with the most bitter sorrow in my heart, when all at once I heard the
sing-song voice of a child in a nearby house.
Whether it was the voice of a boy or a girl I
cannot say, but again and again it repeated the
refrain "Take it and read, take it and read." At
this I looked up, thinking hard whether there
was any kind of game in which children used
to chant words like these, but I could not remember ever hearing them before. I stemmed
my flood of tears and stood up, telling myself
that this could only be a divine command to
open my book of Scripture and read the first
passage on which my eyes should fall.

He happened to have Paul's epistle to the Romans with
him because a friend of his brought it along with him. So he
picked it up to read it because he felt compelled to do. Now,
this isn't the typical way we do Bible study, but Augustine
believed this was what God wanted him to do at this point.
God's sovereign grace was evident in this event.

Has God ever done this with you? Has there been a
time when you felt compelled to read a particular book or
Bible passage, and there was a particular word in it for you?
Augustine got such a word. He went on to say, "I stemmed
my flood of tears and stood up, telling myself that this could
only be a divine command to open my book of Scripture and
read the first passage upon which my eyes should fall. For I
had heard the story of Antony, and I remembered how he had

happened to go into a church while the Gospel was being read and had taken it to as a counsel addressed to himself when he heard the words, 'Go home and sell all that belongs to you. Give it to the poor, and so the treasure you have shall be in heaven; then come back and follow me' (Matthew 19:21)."

That is exactly what Anthony did, and he ultimately became a hermit in the desert. The *Life of Anthony* was a very influential journal that was available at that time. Augustine recalled, "So I hurried back to the place where Alypius was sitting, for when I stood up to move away I had put down the book containing Paul's Epistles. I seized it and opened it, and in silence read the first passage on which my eyes fell." I want to point out how relevant this passage was to Augustine's particular problem. It was absolutely perfect: "Not in reveling and drunkenness, not in lust and wantonness, not in quarrels or rivalries. Rather, arm yourselves with the Lord Jesus Christ; spend no more thought on nature and nature's appetites." This passage from Romans 13 addresses the truth that life is not found in the lust of the flesh, but rather in the Lord Jesus Christ. Augustine then wrote, "I had no wish to read more and no need to do so. For in an instant as I came to the end of the sentence, it was as though the light of confidence flooded into my heart and all the darkness of doubt was dispelled." It was at this point that Augustine recorded that he became a Christian.

Book 9

When Augustine told his mother about his conversion, "she was jubilant with triumph," and she said that she no longer needed anything, as she had completed what she had hoped to accomplish with her life. With regard to this, I want to briefly mention a passage from the ninth book. Shortly before his mother's death, Augustine described a powerful experience they had shared as they traveled back to Africa. They were both leaning from a window that overlooked the garden in the courtyard, and they enjoyed a lengthy discussion on what eternal life might be like.

He then wrote, "I believe that what I am going to tell happened through the secret working of your providence. For we were talking alone together and our conversation was serene and joyful. 'We had forgotten what we had left behind and were intent on what lay before us' (Philippians 3:13). In the presence of truth, which is yourself, we were wondering what the eternal life of the saints would be like, that life which 'no eye has seen, no ear has heard, no human heart conceived' (1 Corinthians 2:9). But we laid the lips of our hearts to the heavenly stream that flowed from your fountain."

He continued,

> Our conversation led us to the conclusion that no bodily pleasure, however great it might be, and whatever earthly light might shed luster upon it, was worthy of comparison, or even of mention, beside the happiness of the life of the saints. As the flame of love burned stronger

in us and raised us higher towards the eternal God, our thoughts ranged over the whole compass of material things in their various degrees, up to the heavens themselves, from which the sun and the moon and the stars shine down upon the earth. Higher still we climbed, thinking and speaking all the while in wonder at all that you have made. At length we came to our own souls and passed beyond them to that place of everlasting plenty, where you feed Israel for ever with the food of truth. There life is that Wisdom by which all these things that we know are made, all things that ever been and all that are yet to be. But that Wisdom is not made: it is as it has always been and as it will be for ever or, rather, I should not say that it *has been* or *will be*, for it simply *is*, because eternity is not in the past or in the future. And while we spoke of the eternal Wisdom, longing for it and straining for it with all the strength of our hearts, for one fleeting instant we reached out and touched it. Then with a sigh, leaving *our spiritual harvest* (Romans 8:23) bound to it, we returned to the sound of our own speech, in which each word has a beginning and an ending.

What a wonderful vision they shared together. Just five days later Monica developed a terrible fever, and then in a few days she was gone. It is a powerful story.

Implications

I want to pull out just a few implications of this material as we close. I would suggest that there are three particular applications that come to my mind, and then I want to give you two significant quotes to conclude. Honesty in self-examination before God is a true virtue. We need to be brutally honest with our flesh, our machinations, our manipulations, and our motivations so that we do not deceive ourselves. We can be honest with our flesh because it is not the deepest part of our being. Believers are new creations, and Christ is in us. He is our hope and our glory. The old things have gone, and the new has come (Colossians 1:27; 2 Corinthians 5:17). As a consequence, therefore, we can become brutally honest with the flesh and practice self-control in the power of the indwelling Christ.

I suggest that, like Augustine, all of us reflect on our spiritual journeys. Perhaps some of us would even benefit from writing it out. Go back to the earliest days of preparation. You may not have done this before. Go back to what could be regarded as your sovereign foundations. Before you knew Jesus, what people and circumstances did God use to woo you and draw you to himself? What desires, passions, and longings did you have? How did those factors affect you in your adolescence? As you move through these types of questions, you can map your own spiritual journey, and it may provide a perspective of gratitude that you otherwise would not have.

A third application is the reminder to habitually call

on the Lord in all your experiences and decisions. In other words, we need to examine whether we have the kind of routine where we hurriedly acknowledge God's presence a few minutes in the morning before we head off to the races and then ignore him until a couple of moments before we go to sleep. If this is the case, we are practical atheists. It is essential for us to involve the Lord in our thoughts, decisions, work, relationships, finances, and every component of our lives. The more we are aware of the Lord's presence, the richer our lives become. God has ordered life in such a way that we can be aware of two levels at once: the earthly level of what we see and feel and touch and taste and hear and also the spiritual level of God's providential working out his will in us and on earth.

Conclusion

Finally, let me share with you what I regard as my favorite passages (besides the one already mentioned that says, "You have made us for yourself and our hearts are restless until they find rest in you"). Two others truly speak to me whenever I read them. One of them is just a little sentence: "The man who serves you best is the one who is less intent on hearing from you what he wills to hear than on shaping his will according to what he hears from you." Here Augustine noted that the people who serve God best are much less interested in hearing from God what they want to hear than they are in shaping their wills toward what God is offering. Instead of shaping our desires on our questions, we should shape our desires on God's answers.

Another favorite passage states, "Give me the grace to do as you command, and command me to do what you will!" This summarizes so much for me. It is God's grace that makes it possible for us to do what he commands. When we invite him to do that, we can then respond as he wants because we are acting in his power and strength and not in the power of our flesh.

Lord, we thank you for your love for us and for this great servant of yours who has so shaped the body of Christ in so many rich and diverse ways. I pray that we might follow his example by being a people who pursue you with a passionate desire to know you and to be known by you. Cause us to be drawn to you so that we may respond to your loving initiatives in our lives. Cause us to be willing to do whatever it takes in order to be more intimate with you so that you become more real to us. We pray these things in Jesus' name and for his glory. Amen.

NOTES

The Pursuit of God

Introduction

A. W. Tozer was an American preacher, author, and modern mystic who gave priority to the lost art of meditation. He was born in 1897 in a small community in Pennsylvania and died in 1963. He authored more than forty books (all but a few were adapted from his sermons), writing *The Pursuit of God* in 1948. He was a self-taught man without much formal education yet became a brilliant scholar who loved to read and reflect. He steeped himself in the literature of the ancient and medieval mystics and found in these people, whom he called "friends of God," kindred spirits—something that he found lacking in the modern evangelicalism of his time.

Tozer was not only a mystic but also a prophet. He exhorted people to know God passionately and intimately, rather than by mere hearsay. He wanted people to know God in the fullness of an experiential apprehension.

Tozer was a remarkable man of God. William F. Bryan, a minister of the Christian and Missionary Alliance—the denomination that Tozer was associated with—said, "I consider Dr. Tozer the most remarkable man of God that I have known personally. In my opinion, his greatest gifts were prophetic insight regarding biblical truth and the nature and state of the evangelical church of his generation. He was respected highly even by those who considered him severe and aloof but to those who knew him he was gracious and kind. I believe Tozer was a lonely man, as many great men of God have been" (James L. Snyder, *In Pursuit of God: The Life of A. W. Tozer* [Camp Hill, PA: Christian Publications, 1994], 3).

In fact, Tozer had very few friends, but this was a deliberate choice to enable him to spend time cultivating a friendship with God. That is not to say that he was aloof, but he didn't allow time for small talk. When he would preach, he had a habit of slipping out before the end of the last hymn, and he would only visit people if they were critically ill. Obviously, it wasn't a positive sign, then, if he did visit someone; and there is a humorous story to that effect. Apparently, Tozer flew back home from an out-of-town speaking engagement; and in the course of the drive from the airport, he was asked to go by the hospital to visit a church elder who was there recovering from minor surgery. Tozer agreed and stopped to visit the man: "When the elder saw Tozer enter his room, he blanched, saying, 'Surely, I am not that sick, am I?' Turning to his wife, also in the room, he asked, 'Are you sure the doctors have told me everything?'" Years later Tozer tried to deny the story, but then weakly admitted, "It could have happened" (211).

Although he was not the most personable pastor, people sought him out as they discovered his spiritual depth. The young Billy Graham regarded him as a spiritual mentor, as did politician Mark Hatfield. Tozer even sustained a running correspondence with the Trappist monk Thomas Merton. This was not characteristic of a fundamentalist Christian and Missionary Alliance pastor, but Tozer was a man who transcended his time. He developed a passionate, purposeful, and God-intoxicated life; and his vibrant relationship with God animated his writings, preaching, and everything he did. He preferred spending time with God rather than people, and he practiced the experiential presence of God.

Aiden Wilson Tozer was raised in a small farming community in western Pennsylvania. At age twenty-two, just five years after his conversion and without any formal theological training, he began what became a forty-four year ministry with the Christian and Missionary Alliance (C&MA). From 1928 until 1959 he served as a prominent pastor of the Southside Alliance Church in Chicago. The last years of his life, he served as pastor of a church in Toronto. Throughout all of those years, he and his wife always lived simply, giving away most of his earnings to those in need.

Tozer's spiritual intuition enabled him to sense error, identify it for what it was, and reject it, all in one decisive act. He effectively ministered to people who were hungry for God. His congregations were never large, yet he delivered powerful sermons from his time spent with the Lord in Scripture and in prayer. He was sought after as a speaker and contributed as a writer to *Alliance Weekly,* later called *Alliance Life,* a publication of the C&MA. He introduced what became known as "Tozer-grams," pithy statements of wisdom and insight.

He never took a vacation and seldom took a day off from ministry. He may have been difficult to live with because of his reclusive disposition. He and his wife had six sons and one daughter, and he harbored an old-school mindset of letting his wife, Aida, take charge of all domestic issues. He was blessed in his marriage to Aida, who kept life in order so that Tozer could devote his time to study and prayer. Tozer's daughter, Rebecca, was born about nine years after the last of his sons, when Tozer was forty-two years old, and apparently she could manipulate him in a way his sons never could. She presented a real challenge to his parenting style, and they became very emotionally close. Even though he remained stern, Rebecca was able to encourage a tender side of his personality that was previously underdeveloped.

Tozer's real strength emanated from his prayer life, and he often commented, "As a man prays, so is he" (5). He was a classic devotional writer, conveying a message that penetrated the soul. His style and strength of expression have continued to attract a growing readership, and he is actually much more popular now than he was in his own time. Speaking about friends and religious leaders who left no room for unhurried reflection or meditation, he said, "Our religious activities should be ordered in such a way as to leave plenty of time for the cultivation of the fruits of solitude and silence" (7). He intuitively went back to the ancient spiritual disciplines at a time well before their current popularity. His preoccupation, his passion, was to practice the presence of God. "Worship," he wrote, "is to feel in your heart and express in some appropriate manner a humbling but delightful sense of admiring awe, astonished wonder and overpowering love in the presence of that most ancient Mystery, that Majesty, which philosophers call the First Cause but which we call our Father in Heaven" (8).

Tozer sought to study the Christian mystics and know the truths they conveyed intimately. He avoided superficial contacts and maintained only a small circle of friends. His authority as a preacher reflected the spiritual authenticity in his own life. He ushered people straight into the presence of God, and people who met him would often say, "There is something about being in that man's presence; I felt as though I was truly in the presence of God."

He would ardently pray about his sermons, which were the fruit of his time invested before God. He even had a special pair of pants he would wear for this purpose. He would take off his suit pants and put on that ragged pair of pants before prostrating himself before the living God. It was in that time of holy awe and wonder that he would welcome the Spirit of God to infuse him and to ravish him. His sermons were steeped in declarations of what he had discovered in prayer. He once put it this way: "Years ago I prayed that God would sharpen my mind and enable me to receive everything He wanted to say to me. I then prayed that God would anoint my head with the oil of the prophet so I could convey it back to people" (160–1). Tozer understood that his messages would not be received by everybody, but his writings speak to those who have a passion to know God and his Word.

The Pursuit of God is a book to be read frequently, perhaps once a year. Each time I read it, I glean new insights, especially in times of spiritual dryness. This is a book I pick up when God seems distant, and it reminds that God is always nearby; he has not moved. Tozer's writings invite us, call us, as the psalmist did, to come away and to taste and to see that God is real, that God is good, and that God is available to us.

In this particular book, Tozer offered encouraging comments that the reader would not have read "this far" if he or she did not already possess godly passions. As he put it, "All the foregoing presupposes true repentance and a full committal of the life to God. It is hardly necessary to mention this, for only persons who have made such a committal will have read this far." He wrote for those who desire a deeper relationship with God and who are interested in substance.

His love of unusual books strikes me. He stipulated that the teachers he chose to instruct him must know God "otherwise than by hearsay," to borrow Thomas Carlisle's phrase. Tozer selected teachers of spiritual authority. Nicholas of Cusa, Fredrick William Faber, and Francois Fenelon were authors whose books he would search for in secondhand bookstores. He amassed a rather unusual library for an evangelical. I have read through a list of the books that most influenced Tozer, and I have made it a point to read them all. Tozer's favorite authors include Richard Rolle, John of the Cross, Thomas à

Kempis, Bernard of Clairvaux, Walter Hilton, and Thomas Kelly. All were friends of God who shaped Tozer's life.

Tozer dearly loved poetry. In fact, the last of his publications is called *The Christian Book of Mystical Verse*. He edited it in 1963, just a few months before his death. This little book contains those poets who fully resonated with Tozer's soul. It is a powerful meditative tool indeed.

I was deeply impressed by the covenant that he composed for his ordination when he was a young man. He made a covenant before God that he later formalized and published in one of the first issues of *Alliance Life*. He said, among other things,

> Lord Jesus, I come to Thee for spiritual preparation. Lay Thy hand upon me. Anoint me with the oil of the New Testament prophet. Forbid that I should become a religious scribe and thus lose my prophetic calling. Save me from the curse that lies dark across the face of the modern clergy, the curse of compromise, of imitation, of professionalism. Save me from the error of judging a church by its size, its popularity or the amount of its yearly offerings. Help me to remember that I am a prophet— not a promoter, not a religious manager but a prophet. Let me never become a slave to crowds. Heal my soul of calm ambitions and deliver me from the itch for publicity.
>
> Save me from the bondage to things. Let me not waste my days puttering around the house. Lay Thy terror upon me, O God, and

> drive me to the place of prayer where I may
> wrestle with principalities and powers and the
> rulers of the darkness of this world. Deliver
> me from overeating and late sleeping. Teach
> me self-discipline that I may be a good soldier
> of Jesus Christ. (Snyder, *Tozer*, pp. 58–59)

Tozer was willing to pay the price because he knew there was the law of reciprocal honor: "Those who honor You, You will also honor." He concluded, "And now, O Lord of heaven and earth, I consecrate my remaining days to Thee; let them be many or few, as Thou wilt. Let me stand before the great or minister before the poor and lowly. That choice is not mine, and I would not influence it if I could. I am Thy servant to do Thy will, and that will is sweeter to me than position or riches or fame. I choose it above all things on earth or in Heaven" (59). These are not the ordinary words of an ordinary man; he understood the manifest presence of God.

I mentioned Tozer's "Tozer-grams" previously, and here are some examples of those taken from Snyder's biography of Tozer:

- The man of true faith may live in the absolute assurance that his steps are ordered by the Lord. For
him misfortune is outside the bounds of possibility.
He cannot be torn from this earth one hour ahead
of the time which God has appointed, and he cannot
be detained on earth one moment after God is done
with him here. He is not a waif of the wide world, a
foundling of time and space, but a saint of the Lord
and the darling of His particular care. (46)

- A world of confusion and disappointment results from trying to believe without obeying. This puts us in a position of a bird trying to fly with one wing folded. (100)

- Religious habits can deceive the possessor as few things can do. As far as I know, a habit and a mud turtle are the only two things in nature that can walk around after they are dead. For instance, many a man has returned thanks at the table faithfully for many years, and yet has never once really prayed from the heart during all that time. The life died out of the habit long ago, but the habit itself persisted in the form of a meaningless mumble. (129)

- It would be well for us if we could learn early the futility of trying to obtain forbidden things by over-persuading God. He will not be thus stampeded. Anything that falls within the circle of His will He gives freely to whosoever asks aright, but not days or weeks of fasting or prayer will persuade Him to alter anything that has gone out of His mouth. (176)

- When God sets out to make a really superior Christian, He is compelled to strip the man of everything that might serve as a false refuge, a secondary trust. He must set the man up to Himself only, or give him up to be a second-rate saint. (194)

The circumstances of writing *The Pursuit of God* are described in the very helpful biography of Tozer, which has been referenced above: *In Pursuit of God: The Life of A. W. Tozer* by James L. Snyder. Snyder was an associate of Tozer's and knew him intimately. He wrote this intriguing account of Tozer's creation of *The Pursuit of God*:

> He was struggling under the increasing pressure of the first of these burdens when he received an invitation to preach in McAllen, Texas—far down toward the Mexican border. He saw in it an opportunity. The long train ride from Chicago would afford him ample time to think and to write. As he boarded the Pullman at the old LaSalle Street Station, Tozer requested of the porter a small writing table for his roomette. There, with only his Bible before him, he began to write. About 9 o'clock PM, the porter knocked on the door. "This is the last call for dinner," he announced. "Would you want me to bring you something to eat?" "Yes," Tozer responded. "Please bring me some toast and tea." With only toast and tea to fortify him physically, Tozer continued to write. He wrote all night long, the words coming to him as fast as he could jot them down. The manuscript was almost writing itself, so full of the subject was he. Early the next morning when the train pulled into McAllen, a rough draft of *The Pursuit of God* was complete. (124)

The Pursuit of God is clearly the product of a man who studied and drank deeply at the well of the Scriptures and of the mystics. The theme of this book is that God is the heart's true longing and that we can only find satisfaction in him. All ten chapters reinforce that concept and address the issue of knowing God not by secondhand accounts of him but by personal and intimate firsthand encounters.

Tozer stressed a concept termed "prevenient grace." This is the idea that God's grace is always previous to our response. The title of this work, therefore, is a pun, for although the book stresses the importance of pursuing an intimate relationship with God, it is, in fact, God who is always first and relentlessly pursuing us. It is God who is in pursuit. As John wrote in 1 John 4:19, "We love because he first loved us" (NIV). Tozer was a firm believer that if a person is called to know God, God is already speaking to that soul, saying, "Come away with me to a quiet place and let us be together. Let us commune and enjoy sweet fellowship. Let us move away from the trials and strains of the world for a season. Let us move away from that."

This is a challenge, is it not, with our frenetic schedules and the din of noise all around us? We hardly understand silence, let alone solitude. A person today must literally plan ahead to enjoy solitude. Yet I recommend that it is something we should pursue vigorously. It is my conviction that we will never regret time spent alone with God, whether that be a morning, or an evening, a whole day, or a more extended period of time. At the end of our journeys, it would be tragic to regret that we wasted a lot of time that we could have spent in cultivating intimacy with the Lord through his Scriptures and in prayer. We are all so involved with this passing world that we often simply forget to make time for what is most important.

Chapter 1

The first chapter of *The Pursuit of God* is called "Following Hard after God." Tozer wrote that even when we are following hard after God, we are already in his hand. God is always previous. He explained, "There must be positive reciprocation," though, and Tozer emphasized the importance of responding to God's loving initiative. Yet we can say no. God, the lover of our souls, can be denied. We can reject and turn away from him.

The heart that responds to God's quiet call will be rewarded because "God is a person." Intimacy can't be achieved in one encounter, but it is "a response of personality to personality," from the "created personalities to the Creating Personality, God." He further explained that it is "the heavenly birth without which we cannot see the Kingdom of God. It is, however, not an end but an inception, for now begins the glorious pursuit."

Tozer understood that salvation is not simply our sins being forgiven and someday going to heaven. He understood that eternal life is in the present tense, and there is a glorious *now* involved in the pursuit of God. He understood that there is a paradox of love—after finding God, we still pursue him. We are satisfied in God, and yet we hunger to know him better. We drink at his well, and yet we still thirst for more understanding.

We see this paradox lived out in David, in Paul, and in many of the great saints through the ages. Tozer stressed, "We have been snared in the coils of a spurious logic which insists that as we have found Him we need no more seek Him." He felt this was a mistake and wrote, "The stiff and wooden quality about our religious lives is a result of our lack of holy desire." This was a key theme for the mystics, and it was a key theme for Tozer—the issue of holy desire.

God wants to be wanted just for himself. Tozer suggested, "We must simplify our approach to Him. We must strip down to essentials (and they will be found to be blessedly few). We must put away all efforts to impress, and come with the guileless candor of childhood. If we do this, without doubt God will quickly respond. . . . There is little that we need other than God Himself. The evil habit of seeking 'God-and' [that is, God plus something else (italics added)] effectively prevents us from finding God in full revelation. . . . We can well afford to make God our All, to concentrate, to sacrifice the many for the One." This is an important theme that runs throughout his writings and throughout the writings of the men and women he read, as well. He wrote, "The man who has God for his treasure has all things in One. Many ordinary treasures may be denied him, or if he is allowed to have them, the enjoyment of them will be so tempered that they will never be necessary to his happiness."

If we are given earthly treasures, we should enjoy them without letting them define us. We should not let the world be so much with us that we cling to it and that it clings to us. That is really what he was saying. He further clarified, "Or if he must see them go, one after one, he will scarcely feel a sense of loss, for having the Source of all things he has in One all the satisfaction, all pleasure, all delight." Tozer understood that whenever we sacrifice and let go of earthly things to get to know God, we will discover that we have gained what is invaluable.

At the end of each chapter, Tozer wrote a little prayer, and, frankly, the prayers alone are worth the price of the book. Here is the first prayer:

> O God, I have tasted Thy goodness, and it has both satisfied me and made me thirsty for more. I am painfully conscious of my need of further grace. I am ashamed of my lack of desire. O God, the Triune God, I want to want Thee; I long to be filled with longing; I thirst to be made more thirsty still. Show me Thy glory, I pray Thee, that so I may know Thee indeed. Begin in mercy a new work of love within me. Say to my soul, "Rise up, my love, my fair one, and come away." Then give me grace to rise and follow Thee up from this misty lowland where I have wandered so long.

That is a powerful prayer, a prayer of passion, the prayer of a man who followed hard after God.

Chapter 2

In the second chapter, called "The Blessedness of Possessing Nothing," Tozer wrote, "The way to deeper knowledge of God is through the lonely valleys of soul poverty and abnegation of all things. The blessed ones who possess the Kingdom are they who have repudiated every external thing and have rooted from their hearts all sense of possessing." Tozer used Abraham as his exemplar, and his interpretation of Abraham's great test is fascinating. He suggested that Abraham might have been on the verge of substituting his precious son for God's love. After all, he had waited many years for the child of promise, and it was through Isaac that the covenant was to be fulfilled. Then God demands that Abraham sacrifice to him that same child of promise, and Abraham unflinchingly obeys.

Tozer then examined why God might have made such a seemingly unreasonable demand. Yet it is at the moment of great testing that Abraham glimpses God in a way he had never before known him. When Abraham offers up his son, "He [God] now says in effect, 'It is all right Abraham. I never intended that you should actually slay the lad. I only wanted to remove him from the temple of your heart that I might reign unchallenged there.'" Tozer continued on to imply that God demonstrated an important principle to Abraham in that moment of faith. Abraham was forced to choose between God and everything else, and when he chose God, he was able to fully enjoy God and everything else, too. Had he chosen Isaac over God, his love for both God and son would most surely have eroded.

So, we have to ask one another a tough question: What is our Isaac? What is it that we cling to and refuse to relinquish? If we are clinging to anything or anyone in lieu of God, the result will be compromise and mediocrity. So, Tozer said that we must root out that thing, that deepest aspiration, so we will desire God above all else. As he put it, Abraham "had everything, but he possessed nothing. There is the spiritual secret. There is the sweet theology of the heart which can only be learned in the school of renunciation. Many books on systematic theology overlook this, but the wise will understand." Tozer observed, "Real treasures are inward and eternal. . . . Everything is safe which we commit to Him, and nothing is really safe which is not so committed." There is a safety in letting loose of temporal things. He went on to say, "Our gifts and talent should also be turned over to Him," because they are really only on loan to us anyway.

He stressed this school of renunciation and noted, "If we are set upon the pursuit of God He will sooner or later bring us to this test." Sooner or later God will test our aspirations. He will test our intentions and will say, "Okay, let's see." It is one thing to think about letting go of some coveted possession, but it is quite another thing to see it taken from us. Our whole future is conditional on the choice we make. It is this concept that animates Tozer's prayer at the end of this chapter:

> Father, I want to know Thee, but my coward heart fears to give up its toys. I cannot part with them without inward bleeding, and I do not try to hide from Thee the terror of the parting. I come trembling, but I do come. Please root from my heart all those things which I have cherished so long and which have become a very part of my living self, so that Thou mayest

enter and dwell there without a rival. Then
shall Thou make the place of Thy feet glorious.
Then shall my heart have no need of the sun
to shine in it, for Thyself wilt be the light of it,
and there shall be no night there.

Chapter 3

In the third chapter, "Removing the Veil," Tozer quoted
Augustine's famous statement from his *Confessions*, "You have
made us for Yourself, O God, and our hearts are restless till
they rest in Thee." Here Tozer addressed the manifest presence of God and God's desire for us to live in him. However,
something seems to separate us from God. Tozer suggested
that this barrier is like the veil in the Old Testament taberna-
cle, which separated the Holy Place from the place where the
priests daily ministered. The Most Holy Place, where God's
glory was revealed, was restricted; only the high priest could
enter annually on the Day of Atonement. Tozer explained
that when Christ died, the veil in the temple in Jerusalem
split from top to bottom, showing that through Christ, we
now have open access to God. (See Hebrews 10:19–20.)

Yet Tozer went on to explain that there are still veils—
veils of our own making, woven of thick strands of the
"self-life." These self-imposed veils prevent us from entering into enjoyment of God himself. He wrote, "The world
is perishing for the lack of the knowledge of God and the
Church is famishing for want of His presence." Tozer went on
to describe this veil concept:

> It is woven of the fine threads of the self-life, the hyphenated sins of the human spirit. . . . To be specific, the self-sins are these: self-righteousness, self-pity, self-confidence, self-sufficiency, self-admiration, self-love and a host of others like them. The grosser manifestations of these sins, egotism, exhibitionism, self-promotion, are strangely tolerated in Christian leaders, even in circles of impeccable orthodoxy. . . . I trust it is not a cynical observation to say that they appear these days to be a requisite for popularity in some sections of the Church visible. Promoting self under the guise of promoting Christ is currently so common as to excite little notice. . . . Self is the opaque veil that hides the face of God from us. . . . We must bring our self-sins to the cross for judgment. . . . Our part is to yield and to trust.

He concluded chapter 3 with this prayer: "Lord, how excellent are Thy ways and how devious and dark are the ways of man. Show us how to die, that we may rise again to newness of life. Rend the veil of our self-life from top down as Thou didst rend the veil of the Temple. We would draw near in full assurance of faith. We would dwell with Thee in daily experience here on this earth so that we may be accustomed to the glory when we enter Thy Heaven to dwell with Thee there."

Tozer was saying to get ready. Life is brief. We must welcome God's presence because all of life is about knowing him. That is what eternity will be about as well—knowing him. Heaven will not be a static affair at all, but an intimate, relational, dynamic time of growth in the corporate context of fellowship, communion, beauty, and adventure. The ultimate source of pleasure will be enjoying the presence of the One from whom all pleasures come (Psalm 16:11).

Remember what C. S. Lewis said in *The Screwtape Letters*, when Uncle Screwtape was advising Wormwood: "Never forget that when we are dealing with any pleasure in its healthy and normal and satisfying form, we are, in a sense, on the Enemy's ground. I know we have won many a soul through pleasure. All the same, it is His invention, not ours. He made the pleasures: all our research so far has not enabled us to produce one" ([New York: HarperCollins, 2001], 44). In other words, all pleasures come from God. It would be foolish for us to suppose, therefore, that by yielding to him we could deny ourselves joy. God is not the enemy of our joy; in fact, he is the wellspring of all true joy. We will learn this as we grow in faith and let go of those things, appetites, and desires that deceive us into believing that God is some kind of a cosmic sadist or killjoy who wants us to be miserable. This deception is really an unbiblical, demonic notion, indeed.

Chapter 4

This next chapter is entitled "Apprehending God," and here Tozer addressed "the inferential character of the average man's faith in God," and he expressed it this way: "For millions of Christians, nevertheless, God is no more real than He is to the non-Christian. They go through life trying to love an ideal and to be loyal to a mere principle." It is difficult to fall in love with a principle or an ideal. We do not really know God if we have only reasoned about him from the facts of revelation. Tozer discussed the need to apprehend God in a spiritual way and to come into his actual living presence. He asserted, "The worshipping heart does not create its Object. It finds Him here when it wakes from its moral slumber in the morning of its regeneration. . . . The world of sense intrudes upon our attention day and night for the whole of our lifetime."

He warned about the "intrusive ubiquity of visible things." That is the problem with the world—it never lets go of us and continually reinforces the visible over the invisible. Thus, faith is required to pursue those things that are not now seen. The world causes us to shift our interest from the eternal to the temporal, and yet the Scriptures invite us to move the other way around. Tozer argued, "The visible becomes the enemy of the invisible; the temporal, of the eternal." According to him, "every man must choose his world. . . . We must avoid the common fault of pushing the 'other' world into the future."

Tozer was not some "pie in the sky, by and by" kind of saint, but rather he noted, "It is not future, but present. It parallels our familiar physical world, and the doors between the two worlds are open." He was saying that the quality of the eternal and the invisible can be infused into our daily experience.

The prayer at the end of this chapter is very brief: "O God, quicken to life every power within me, that I may lay hold on eternal things. Open my eyes so that I may see; give me acute spiritual perception; enable me to taste Thee and to know that Thou art good. Make Heaven more real to me than any earthly thing has ever been."

Chapter 5

Under the title "The Universal Presence," Tozer discussed "the divine immanence." This particular chapter influenced me in the writing of my first book in 1974. I read *The Pursuit of God* twice that year because I believed it would help me better grasp some of the mysteries of the God I was conveying in the book. In that work I examined such mysteries as the God-man, the Trinity, divine sovereignty versus human responsibility, God's relation to time and space, immanence versus transcendence, omnipresence versus localization, and the nature of the resurrection body. Tozer's writings helped me immensely in this process. For example, speaking of God's transcendence, he wrote, "He is transcendent above all His works even while He is immanent within them. No point is nearer to God than any other point." He continued, "The Presence and the manifestation of the Presence are not the same." God can be present without us experiencing his presence. It is as Jacob said, "Surely the LORD is in this place; and I knew it not" (Genesis 28:16 KJV). At first Jacob did not recognize his location as a holy place, but after his dream, he named it the house of God.

We experience something similar when we become aware of God's manifest presence where we are and realize that "our pursuit of God is successful just because He is forever seeking to manifest Himself to us. . . . There is no idea of the physical distance involved in the concept. It is not

a matter of miles but of experience." And so, Tozer defined
the cultivation of the art of "spiritual receptivity." He talked
about the lifelong habit of spiritual response and how this
spiritual receptivity can be cultivated by spiritual exercise,
declaring that "it may be increased by exercise or destroyed
by neglect."

This correlation is obvious on the physical level, and
it ought to point us to spiritual truth as well. Our current
habits of diet and exercise play a large role in determining
what our lives will be like five years from now. We know that
we cannot suddenly become a model of physical prowess.
Rather, we must engage in daily disciplines that move us in
that direction. This principle is painfully obvious in the material world, but we somehow miss it in the spiritual realm.
We wrongly suppose that a little time here and five minutes
there will bring us into intimacy with God. Tozer warned us
to think again.

Tozer felt it would be a sad thing for us to come to
the end of our life journey and realize that God was only a
stranger or a theological precept rather than the lover of our
souls. Obedience and humility are the keys to this process.
He wrote, "We have accepted one another's notions, copied
one another's lives and made one another's experiences the
model for our own." His prayer following this chapter is
appropriate. "O God and Father, I repent of my sinful preoccupation with visible things. The world has been too much
with me. Thou hast been here and I knew it not. I have been
blind to Thy Presence. Open my eyes that I may behold Thee
in and around me. For Christ's sake. Amen."

Chapter 6

In the chapter "The Speaking Voice," Tozer argued that God is not someone who merely spoke once and then retreated into silence. Actually, there is a sense in which what is *said* accounts for what is *so*: God *said*, and now it is *so*. Therefore, the *so* is the continuous presence of the *said*. This makes the Bible alive, not dead. It is not an end in itself but a vehicle by which to know the One who is alive. Tozer invited us to "come at once to the open Bible expecting it to speak to you."

In other words, we should present ourselves, unreservedly, before God as we open the Bible, saying, "Behold, now, your servant is here." In so doing, we invite the fountain of God's fullness into our own soul. Tozer's ending prayer is this: "O Lord, teach me to listen. The times are noisy and my ears are weary with the thousand raucous sounds which continually assault them. Give me the spirit of the boy Samuel when he said to Thee, 'Speak, for thy servant heareth.' Let me hear Thee speaking in my heart. Let me get used to the sound of Thy voice, that its tones may be familiar when the sounds of earth die away and the only sound will be the music of Thy speaking voice."

Chapter 7

Here in "The Gaze of the Soul," Tozer explained faith as the organ of the soul as well as "the gaze of the soul on a saving God." He spoke about the nature of faith and agreed with Thomas à Kempis that we cannot fully define it: "I would rather exercise faith than know the definition thereof." However, he said, "Believing is directing the heart's attention to Jesus."

He spoke of a spiritual reflex in which "the heart's intention is to gaze forever on Jesus." He wrote, "Like the eye which sees everything in front of it and never sees itself, faith is occupied with the Object upon which it rests and pays no attention to itself at all. While we are looking at God we do not see ourselves—blessed riddance." As we take our eye off ourselves and focus on Jesus, we will be able to know God better. Tozer continued, saying, "[A man] will experience real relief when he stops tinkering with his soul and looks away to the perfect One. While he looks at Christ the very things he has so long been trying to do will be getting done within him."

Therefore, "faith is a redirecting of our sight," and "the sweet language of experience is 'Thou God seest me.'" Tozer spoke about the simplicity of faith. The prayer at the end of this chapter says, "O Lord, I have heard a good word inviting me to look away to Thee and be satisfied. My heart longs to respond, but sin has clouded my vision till I see Thee but dimly. Be pleased to cleanse me in Thine own precious blood, and make me inwardly pure, so that I may with unveiled eyes gaze upon Thee all the days of my earthly pilgrimage. Then shall I be prepared to behold Thee in full splendor in the day when Thou shall appear to be glorified in Thy saints and admired in all them that believe."

Chapter 8

The essence of "Restoring the Creature-Creator Relation" is an exhortation that we must make up our minds that we are going to exalt God above all else. When we do that, we step out of the world's parade: "Let the average man be put to the proof on the question of who is above, and his true position will be exposed. Let him be forced into making a choice between God and money, between God and men, between God and personal ambition, God and self, God and human love, and God will take second place every time. Those other things will be exalted above. However the man may protest, the proof is in the choices he makes day after day throughout his life."

Here Tozer examined how we can move in this direction. He wrote, "Let no one imagine that he will lose anything of human dignity by this voluntary sell-out of his all to his God." We must come to the point where we take the profound risk of offering ourselves fully to God, with no small print on the contract. This is a terrifying moment, but unless we move into that total abnegation of surrender—which is really an affirmation of God's benevolence toward us—we will never move beyond mediocrity.

In this chapter Tozer reminded us that Jesus said, "My Father will honor the one who serves me" (John 12:26 NIV). When reflecting on these words, Tozer wrote, "The man of God set his heart to exalt God above all." This is a profound and perceptive thought. I have noticed that David and many other biblical characters were not perfect saints. Yet God graciously poured on his servants blessings untold, as if over-looking their weaknesses and failures. Why? Because they pursued him. Because they longed to know him despite their imperfections. Tozer went on to say, "The man of God set his heart to exalt God above all; God accepted his intention as fact and acted accordingly. Not perfection, but holy intention made the difference." That is a phrase that speaks to me. God is not looking for perfection. He is looking for holy inten-tions. It is that which pleases the heart of God. As Thomas Merton put it in his insightful prayer, "The desire to please you does in fact please you" (Thomas Merton, *Thoughts in Solitude* [New York: Farrar, Strauss and Giroux, 1999], 79).

Tozer also addressed the dilemma that "the desire for honor among men made belief impossible." Our lives call into question which audience we are playing to. Are we seek-ing to impress other people, or are we seeking to please the almighty God?

There is a powerful prayer at the end of this chapter. Tozer prayed that God would be "exalted over my posses-sions . . . over my friendships . . . above my comforts . . . over my reputation." This is a prayer we might not want to pray unless we are really serious about honoring God above all else.

Chapters 9 and 10

The subjects of the last two chapters are meekness and rest. Here Tozer described the world's value system as an inversion of the biblical value system. He wrote, "The exact opposite of the virtues in the Beatitudes are the

very qualities which distinguish human life and conduct.
. . . Instead of poverty of spirit we find the rankest kind
of pride; instead of mourners we find pleasure seekers;
instead of meekness, arrogance; instead of hunger after
righteousness we hear men saying, 'I am rich and increased
with goods and have need of nothing.'" He concluded with
the assertion that we must be delivered from the burden of
pride, pretense, and artificiality and surrender ourselves to
Christ. By doing so we will find a blessed relief from much
deception, and we will discover the blessing of childlike
faith. Tozer's closing prayer was an appeal for deliverance:
"Deliver me from the urge to compete with another for a
place or prestige or position. Deliver me from pose and
pretense. . . . Help me to forget myself and to find my
true peace in beholding Thee. That Thou mayest answer this
prayer I humble myself before Thee. Lay upon me Thy easy
yoke of self-forgetfulness that through it I may find rest."

Finally, in the last chapter, "The Sacrament of Living,"
Tozer observed that Jesus lived among people with a restful
poise. He had a great mission to accomplish, but he was never
in a hurry to do so. There is something significant about this.
Tozer defined a sacrament as an "external expression of an
inward grace." He argued that every act of life can have a
sacramental dimension, saying, "We must offer all our acts
to God and believe that he accepts them. . . . Let us practice
the fine art of making every work a priestly ministration."
There is no sacred-secular distinction. In fact, every act can
potentially be an act of worship. Eleven o'clock on Monday
morning can be as sacred as eleven o'clock on Sunday morning; it depends entirely on the motive: "It is not what a man

does that determines whether his work is sacred or secular, but it is *why* he does it. The motive is everything. Let a man sanctify the Lord God in his heart and he can thereafter do no common act."

I will close with this final prayer from the book.

> Lord, I would trust Thee completely; I would be altogether Thine; I would exalt Thee above all. I desire that I feel no sense of possessing anything outside of Thee. I want constantly to be aware of Thy overshadowing Presence and to hear Thy speaking Voice. I long to live in restful sincerity of heart. I want to live so fully in the Spirit that all my thought may be as sweet incense ascending to Thee and every act of my life may be an act of worship. Therefore I pray in the words of Thy great servant of old, "I beseech Thee so for to cleanse the intent of mine heart with the unspeakable gift of Thy grace, that I may perfectly love Thee and worthily praise Thee."

Application

We may not be mystics or prophets, but let me suggest that by God's grace we can move from holy intention to holy action. Do you have a desire to desire God? Do you have a longing to follow after him? Do you have a hunger to hunger after him? Then, thank God for it, and start with where you are today. Your loving Savior will multiply your obedient desires like he multiplied the loaves and fish. I believe that through the grace of God we are called to an ever-increasing awareness of his presence. We are called to passion, to single-minded focus, to radical trust and obedience, and to spend significant time with God.

My desire for all of us is to seek to know God better, to spend the time requisite to becoming intimate with the Lord so that we can hear his voice, not as hearsay but by direct experience.

> Lord, we pray that you would call us ever to your loving voice, that we may be a people who pursue you with a passion and a purpose. We pray for the grace of holy desire, and give us the intention of being pleasing to you. We ask, Lord, that we may seek you and long to know you, that we would follow hard after you and realize that in doing so we are responding to your loving overtures and initiatives in our lives. We pray in Christ's name. Amen.

1-800 7259253
1945

NOTES

888 634 4434 Comcast

Serial # PAFR00409953

TOSHIBA
1-800 631-3881
Model NOMW24F11
Serial # 89788132A